e 2001

GAMES

SLIM PEOPLE

PLAY

Winning the "Slim and Trim" Game

For Greater Health & Vitality

L. Michael Hall, Ph.D.
2001

ISBN Number: 1-890-001-201

Published by:
   Neuro-Semantics® Publications
   P.O. Box 8
   Clifton, CO. 81520 USA
   (970) 523-7877

Printed By:
   Action Printing
   Jerry Kucera, Owner
   516 Fruitvale Court, Unit C
   Grand Jct. CO. 81504
   (970) 434-7701
   Actionpres@aol.com

Cover Designed and Created by *Doug Clary*
   Action Printing
   Grand Jct. CO. 81504

Web Sites:
   www.neurosemantics.com
   www.runyourownbrain.com

RECOMMENDATIONS

A manuscript of this work was sent out in January, 2001 to 15 individuals in six countries with a request for them to put it to the test. Many did. Here are a few results.

"It's been about six months since I began applying the principles in this book, and I'm thrilled to report that I have maintained the original weight loss and added 50 pounds to that figure. I'm at my ideal weight now and feeling lighter and more energetic than I have in 20 years. The best part is that I haven't had to buy expensive machines, eat a wacky diet, or give up eating out at my favorite restaurants with friends. I've just changed the Games I play around food and exercise so I can win and have a lot more fun. Thanks, Dr. Hall!"

> Tom Carroll, Performance Consultant/Coach/Trainer
> Austin, Texas
> http://www.abilitynow.com

"When I began reading, my life was under lots of stress from work, a son just graduating from high school, etc. ... I was getting increasingly frustrated. ... In the initial month I lost 13 pounds, which I have kept off. That goes contrary to my normal pattern of twenty years of 'summer loss, winter gain.' But more than that, I have changed life-long thought patterns which have increased my sense of physical and emotional well-being. The most incredible thing is that instead of running from conflict, I have dived into it to resolve it."

> Pr. John LaMunyon
> Holy Trinity Lutheran Church
> Ephrata, WA.

"Losing weight is a heavy subject that overwhelms many of us. By turning the process into *Games*, Michael Hall has taken a lot of the weight off of weight control. When you understand the Games and know the rules, the Games become fun. If a Game is not fun, refuse to play it and find another one. That simple shift in thinking has done wonders for me and my clients with 'weight problems.' Playing Hall's Game can truly turn you into a 'Survivor.'"

> Peter O'Dell, M.A.
> Success Easy NLP Hypnosis Center
> Boca Raton, Florida
> Success@qth.com

GAMES SLIM PEOPLE PLAY

PREFACE

The Games you play with food (eating) and movement (exercising) determines the Wins and/or Loses that you'll experience.

- So *what* Games have you been playing?
- What Games will you play *today?*

We all play Games because of the way our minds-and-bodies work. There's an old saying, "As we think, so we are." Here we apply that using more modern language and understanding.

> *As we frame (or set frames), so we experience, that is, so we play out the Games set forth in those frames.*

I don't know *what Games* you have been playing with food. I only know that you have been playing "Games." These Games constitute the regular and dependable *set of actions, feelings, and thoughts* you use as you engage and relate to food, eating, and exercising. Such are your Food Games and your Exercise Games.

What Food Games have you been playing? Perhaps:

"I Eat to Feel Loved and Rewarded" Game.

The "Eating is so Relaxing and Fun" Game.

"To Say 'No' to Certain Food is Deprivation" Game.

I also do not I know if you've been playing *healthy and vitalizing Games,* Games that give you such payoffs as looking and feeling good or whether you've been playing foolish Games that undermine your best efforts to take control of your eating and exercising. I don't know if the Games you've been playing actually work for energy and vitality or whether they leave you feeling bloated, heavy, and de-energized. To know that, I would have to ask some other questions:

- Do you like the Games that you've been playing with food, eating, or exercising?
- Have those Games provided you the payoff of the kind of body, energy, and vitality that you want?
- Would you like to play some new Games?
- Would you be willing to learn to play new Games?
- Would you like to refine and exchange some of the old eating and exercising Games for some that will put you in charge of yourself?

- Would you like to become willing to tell some of the old food Games to go to hell?

Why the Dieting Game Does Not Work

Let me tell you about Jenny.

Jenny was one of the fifteen people who "tried out" this book to see if the model worked. When she told me about her situation, she said that she had been trying to lose weight and keep it off for years. She described how she had tried numerous programs, TOPS, Weight Watchers, Jenny Craig, and others. It wasn't that she didn't *know what* to do, how to eat right or know what behavioral changes to make. She knew. And she knew it well.

A few years back, she had given up dieting because of the yo-yo effect that she had begun to suffer.

"I suddenly realized that nine months after any new program, I was heavier. A light came on. I realized that *dieting* itself was the problem!" she said.

It was certainly part of the problem. Above and beyond the activity of dieting were all of the frames of mind she used to have about dieting. These included such frames as:

- The problem is food.
- The problem is eating too much.
- The problem is eating the wrong things.
- the problem is me.
- Etc.

The problem actually was *the very way she was thinking* about eating and dieting. Her mental frames were contributing to her ineffectiveness.

Food Games

Jenny's story explains why this book is about Games—the *Frame Games* that we play. What in the world is a *Frame Game?* This phrase describes the two key facets of every experience:

- *Games:* The actual set of actions and behaviors that we engage in. What we actually *do*. What we *say*, even what we *feel*. Looked at from the outside, these are our Games. Some people eat everything in sight. That's their Game. Others have to clean their plate. That's their Game.

- *Frames:* The ideas in our heads, our beliefs, values, understandings, etc. that establish the Rules of the Games, the Game Set-up. Some of the mental Frames in our heads that set up a Game are simple and direct, "Clean your plate; there are starving children in.... India, Africa, China ..." Other Frames are more subtle and covert. For example, eating a sweet after a meal seems like and feels like a reward. Perhaps sweets were connected to "being a good boy or girl" during childhood and we still have this as our *frame of reference.*

Now while it may seem like the problems we have with weight, body size and shape, over-eating, obesity, lack of fitness, etc. are strictly behavioral problems, they are not. The Games we play are but the expressions of our mental Frames. We play the Games that we do because of the Rules and Understandings that we have in our heads. That's why we trying to change things at the behavioral level without changing the Rules of the Game in our minds seldom works. As long as we *think* the way we do about Food and Exercise, as long as we use the frames of references that we do, we will find it hard to *not* play those Games. At the level of our everyday experience, it seems (feels) that we are destined for those Games.

But that's the lie. That's the deception. We are *not* destined for those Games, or any particular Games for that matter. We play those Games because we know how to play those Games and because we have played those Games for many years. We're familiar with them. Those Games make sense to us, even though they might be destructive in terms of long-term health.

Jenny learned something new in *Games Slim People Play.* She mainly learned a new way to think about food and exercise. When she came upon *Games,* she had already quit the Dieting Game. But she had not learned how to play the Life-Style Game. She didn't have the necessary Frames to set that Game up. Also, she had not learned how to stop playing the Blame Game and to recognize that paradoxically, the

Acceptance Game, the Sensory Eating Game, and the Food for Fuel Game would give her a new handle on things.

Those were some of the new Games she had to learn. And learn it she did. In a 3 month period, she lost 20 pounds and then maintained her new weight. But she did more. She began playing the exercise games so that she has been tightening her muscles and raising her metabolism. It's a whole new lifestyle and she doesn't think in terms of *how little to eat*, she thinks in terms of *what to eat that supports her vitality*.

> "It's like an entirely different way to live. I used to be so conscious of food. Food was always on my mind, I was always thinking about what *not* to eat, what I *should not* eat. I don't even think that way anymore. Now I focus on what will give me energy and vitality."

This explains one of my primary purposes in this book. Namely, I hope to give you *an entirely new way to think* about, and then relate to, eating, exercising, food, weight control, etc. In the vein of the current writings about *dieting no more* and about changing your whole orientation toward the subject of being fit and slim, this book will put into your hands all of the pieces you need to totally take control of fitness and weight control, namely:

- A new map about how to effectively think about the Game of eating and exercising—new Frames of Mind.
- The motivation to play a new Game, to take charge of these areas of life.
- The patterns or processes that will allow you to play a whole new Game and maintain that Game so that it becomes truly *lifestyle eating and exercising*.

Why have I have written with an emphasis on Food Games and Exercise Games? There are several reasons and central among those reasons is this:

The Games We Play
Determine the Way We Live Our Lives
and the Quality of our Lives.

The very *quality* of your life: your health, your energy level, your vitality, your stamina, your fitness, your looks, your emotions, your thinking, etc., is determined by the *quality* of your Games. So if you want to improve the quality of your life, learn to play more Quality Games. And to do that, you'll need some Quality Frames of Mind.

Warning: The New Games are no Panacea

Several of the 15 people I sent the original manuscript did *not* succeed. Why not? Some of them did not even finish reading the first chapter. One person told me that she was looking for a "magical ah-ha!" and when she didn't find it in the first few pages, she lost interest.

Now that's a Frame of Mind that will kill any new interest and undermine long term persistence, commitment, and resilience. Entertain that frame of mind and it will set up the Impatient Game, the Failure to Follow-Through Game, the Jumping Around Dabbling in Lots of Things, but Mastering Nothing Game.

That's why this book is *not* for everyone. If you want to play some of the same old Games with food and refuse to give up those Games, then this book will not work for you. Actually, no book will *work* for you, we are the ones who have to *use* a book, a model, a way of understanding to *change* our lives.

There's no magical panacea here. Unlike the promises you see in the tabloids, you will *not* lose weight while you sleep with no effort. It's those kinds of frames that force you to play the Games that you do—the Games that will keep you over-weight, unfit, stressed, distracted, etc. Thumb through Chapter 8 if you want to know about the Games that will absolutely sabotage your health, fitness, and slimness. Do not buy this book if you *want* to play those Games, or if you want to play the Whining Victim Game, which says,

> "But I tried... I even tried this latest thing on Frame Games and it didn't work either!"

Save your money.

Save your money also if you still operate from the childish magical thinking that motivates the game that so many people *wish* to play, which says,

> *"There ought to be some quick, easy, and effortless way to have*

great fitness, marvelous energy level, and look marvelous!"
Your body doesn't work that way. It never has; it never will. If you are of that frame of mind, it will only make matters worse. It will put you on the now famous dieting "yo-yo." It will undermine your best efforts and add fat in all the spots you don't want or need more fat.

You can master the *Frame Games for fitness and weight management* described in this book if, and only if, you will do the following:

- Assume ownership for all of your mental frames and behavioral Games.
- Devote the time and energy to read and practice the processes. Yes, the book will not read itself, you have to do that, *and* you have to *apply* what you read.
- Give yourself permission to learn entirely new Games.
- Be kind and gentle with yourself regarding your current condition (playing the Judgment Game will not only hurt, it will sabotage your best efforts.
- Be willing to learn how to say *"No!"* to some of the old Games and to refuse those seductive calls.
- Be willing to allow yourself to look great, feel good, and enjoy the energy and vitality that can be yours (this means putting a stop to the "But do I really deserve it?" Game).

Throughout the first part of the book I have focused on food and eating. That is *not* because merely playing a new food Game is sufficient in itself. It is not. Every successful long-term program for weight loss involves exercise as well. You have to incorporate more activity into your daily life to increase your cardio-vascular fitness and to raise your metabolic rate for fat-burning.

Oh yes, one last thing. You will have to *use your intelligence* as you read this book. I have no plans to patronize you or to spoon-feed you the ideas here.

Why not? Why not simplify it and write it for a seventh-grade reading level? I have a reason for this, and I will share it with you, but that's yet to come and if you have the courage to follow your dream about being fit and thin... come with me and we'll play a brand new Game. And it will be a fun one. Unless, of course, you like being fat and out-of-shape.

[By the way, as a semantic device, I will use several linguistic features that may seem strange at first. "Etc." is one of them. Coming from General Semantics, this refers to a semantic device that helps convey the idea that "there's a lot more to be listed, mentioned, or said" about this. In this, *"etc."* challenges the black-and-white dogmatism that assumes that "the last word about this has been spoken." Also, you'll find a series of dots from time to time in the Games, this means to slow down, take your time, experience the words and their references ...]

BEGINNING ORIENTATION

Consider the *frame* and *frameworks* that govern your thinking, perceiving, and responding regarding food and activity at this very moment. As you do, let me tell you something that is both frightening and exciting.

Those frames work! Yet, to what end do they work?

Do they give you the kind of control over your eating and exercising that you want?

Do they empower your body and mind with the kind of energy and power that makes life an adventure?

Do they enable you to live comfortably in your body with grace, ease, and energy?

The problem that we have with eating, weight management, and staying healthy does not lie with food. *Food* is not the problem when it comes to eating, gaining, losing, or maintaining a healthy weight. Food is just food. Our problems with food arise from *how* we relate to it and to the process of eating itself. The problems we experience occurs when we *eat* for the wrong reasons. And, eating for the wrong "reasons," of course, takes us to our *frames* of mind. It creates *Psycho-Eating*.

- What's your frame of reference when you eat, diet, exercise, think about food, wish you could lose some weight, etc.?
- How much importance do you give to eating?
- What frames of mind (thoughts, ideas, memories, etc.) prevent you from taking control of your eating and exercising?
- What frame of mind would you have to put yourself into in order to take charge of your weight and fitness?
- How long do you think losing weight/ gaining weight, and becoming health and fit will take?
- How patient or impatient are you about this?
- Who (if anyone) do you compare yourself with?
- How much do you feel you deserve to be at your best, look your best, feel your best?

The same principle applies to exercise. The problems that we have with fitness, health, or weight do not involve having or not having the equipment, time, and/or motivation to exercise. If we have difficulties here, the problem lies in our *frame-of-reference* about exercise, activity, movement, effort, and that nasty word, "discipline."

You are not the problem. The experience is not the problem. *The frame is the problem!*

This explains it. What will happen **if** we do not address our frames? Without addressing the driving frames, the prcblems we have with eating and exercising, staying vigorous, fit, and slim will continue. We think they rise and fall according to our circumstances, genetics, family heritage, nature, finances, etc. So we go from diet to diet, from one exercise program to another, and one fad to another. Most of them do work; at least they work for awhile. Then cur frames re-assert themselves, and we're back where we started. If you've had enough of *that*, then it's time to understand our frames, the Frame Games that we play. And, learn how to both detect and transform them. This is what you will find as the heart of this book.

Questions for Your Frame Games Slim Notebook

If you really want to play a new and enhancing Game with food, get a notebook, designate it as your *Slim & Fit Game Book,* and use it to answer the sets of questions that you will find in the following chapters. They are usually in bullet format as below. Do this to play the Game of Awareness in order to play the Game of Choice and Empowerment.

* Have you decided to lighten up and become more fit and energetic?
* Why do you want to do this?
* How would that be important and valuable to you?
* What other reasons do you have for this?
* Could anything stop you from doing this?
* What has sabotaged you in the past?
* What resources do you now have that will address those old sabotages?
* Who will you become as you do this?
* Who will you become when you have fully succeeded in this?

- Will you continue and turn it into your lifestyle?
- Could anything stop you from making it your way of being in the world?

HOW TO BEGIN

For many years I have worked with hundreds of individuals who wanted to make a change. During that time I've discovered something most incredible about we humans when it involves—

- *Changing* habits of mind, emotion, and body
- Beginning a new process, or
- Putting bad habits away.

What? Namely, that most people don't really know *how to properly begin the process of making personal changes or transformations*. Do you?

HOW *NOT* TO BEGIN

Most of us attempt to *begin new things* in entirely wrong ways. When most people attempt a new beginning, they co one or more of the following things:

- We **overwhelm** ourselves with all that we have to do, with how far we have to go, with all the work and struggle it's going to take, etc. And in *that* frame of mind, no wonder we sabotage our best plans.

- We **begin doubting** if we can do it from the start. "Can I really do this?" "I don't think I can pull this off." We discount the small steps we take and begin questioning if we really want to do it. Then we question ourselves.

- We start **excusing** ourselves with fancy "reasons" for our weight. "It runs in the family." "It's my genes." "I just look at a cake and gain weight." This leads to **blaming** ("If they just wouldn't entice me with all of the fast food on television.").

- We **evaluate** and judge from minute to minute and don't give the new processes times to work. Feeling impatient, we become critical and demanding. So we judge and criticize every step of the process and bring lots of negative emotions to the process itself.

If you start with any of those *Mind Games*, they will defeat you before you get started. Some of them will *not* even let you get started. If you continue to play these *Frame Games*, you'll achieve nothing except feel bad about feeling powerless and feel the need to go bury your sorrows in some ice cream.

All of that describes how *not* to begin. If you "run your brain" with those kinds of thoughts or that kind of thinking, you will effectively defeat you making a change even before you begin. What can you do? Now's the time for some of your God-given *Stubbornness*. Now's the time to get as mad as hell at those Mind Games your brain is running—and put your foot down. After all, who's in charge, you or your grey matter?

HOW TO BEGIN —

To begin, I want you to play some brand new *Mind Games* (Frame of Mind Games). It doesn't matter whether you agree with me at this point, or whether you think it will work (ah, the Doubting Game again!), or whether you think you can pull it off (ah, the Self-Doubting frame of mind!), or any other excuse that you can invent. Just because you're skilled in Inventing Excuses doesn't mean that you have to keep playing that Game.

Here's what I want you to do. I want you to read the following lines... then write them down in your own hand-writing (are you beginning to make an excuse for *not* doing that?), then I want you to look someone in the face and utter the statements.

- I'm in the process of changing my Frame of Mind. I'm going to play a new Frame Game with regard to food and activity. I am going to take charge of running my own brain. When I get the fat out of my head—the fat will begin to evaporate from of my body.
- I only need to do one small thing every day. I will stubbornly refuse to overwhelm myself with this new Game. Every little thing I do *counts*.
- I stubbornly refuse to play the old Game of excuse making and blaming. I stick things in my mouth because of the old frames of mind that I've developed

and step by step, day by day, I will develop new frames of mind.

- I will play these new Games in a kind and gentle way as I accept where I am now and enjoy the process of change itself.   Getting there is most of the fun.

OVERVIEW
Games Slim People Play

This book is about *Games*. It's about the Weight Management Games that the experts play that enable them to succeed to stay slim—trim and physically alive and vital. It's about the Games that we can learn to play to replicate the success of such people. In doing that, the book is about how those who have found the secret think about the Slimming Games, and how to replicate the frames of mind that govern them.

Why?

To become much more productive and efficient in the Games that we play. Accordingly, this book is about setting new frames of mind and refusing the old frames and the old Games that undermine success.

In *Part I,* we focus on *Figuring Out Frame Games.* This presents the idea of slimming and fitness as "Games" and is the only theoretical part of the book. In this section I will introduce and describe *Frame Games* and how to shift your thinking about your weight, body, eating, exercising, etc., in terms of frames and Games. This sets the stage for everything else: how to detect and identify the Games, how to appreciate the driving power of our mental frames and not get seduced by thinking that they are real.

Part II describes the most foundational Games—the Games that make for personal effectiveness in every realm. *Games for Personal Empowerment* establish the foundation for excellence and expertise in every field, personal, business, athletics, finances, relationship, etc.

Part III describe the Games that allow us to use our power to refuse the seduction of the old Games. In this section we focus on developing awareness about Food Games, identify the Games that do not work, Slaying the Dragons of Stupidity that trick and deceive u, and playing Games that retire the Old Games.

Part IV then gets down to business, to the actual Slimming Games that make for excellence in the business of forming and shaping our bodies so that we use them as vehicles to express ourselves.

A Template for the Games

While I have a more thorough model for thinking about Games in Chapter 3 and have two worksheets there for more extensive Frame Analysis, I have used the following template as a simple way to think about the Games in the following chapters. It follows from what we mean when we talk about a set of actions and interactions as a "Game."

- *The Name* and *the Description* of the Game: What is the Game, how does it work? Does the Game enhance or limit?
- *The Rules* of the Game: How is the Game set up, structured, who plays the Game, when, etc.?
- *The Cues* of the Game: What are the questions that elicit the Game, the terms that reveal the Game? What triggers recruit us to playing the Game?
- *The Payoff* of the Game: What are the benefits, values, and outcomes of the Game?

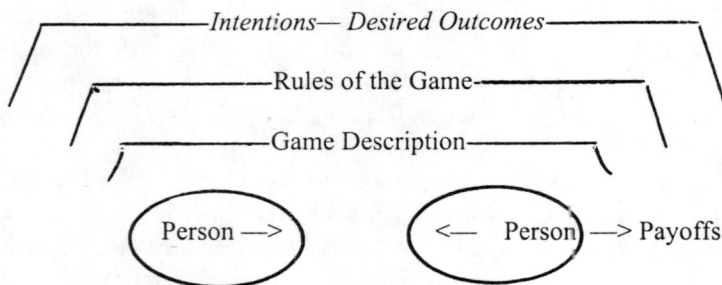

Intentions— Desired Outcomes

Rules of the Game

Game Description

Person —>   <— Person —> Payoffs

Cues for the Games

Toxic or Empowering?

It doesn't matter what we call a Game, I've invented lots of insightful as well as silly titles in the following pages and I invite you to do the same with the Games you play. What matters is whether *they work for you or against you.* You need to know both. Those who are successful in reaching their outcomes do. It's not enough to know the positive, wonderful Games that you want to play and want to say "Yes!" to. Frequently, we can't say a thunderous "Yes!" to what we want until we've said an equally impactful "Hell, No!" to the Games that undermine and sabotage our best efforts.

It's for this reason that I will constantly be contrasting *Bad Game/ Good Game* in the following pages. Your clarity on toxic or enriching will give you the personal power to *cut* (de-*cision*) a clear path toward your desired outcomes. It will also empower you to stand strong and firm when the toxic Games put on a seductive show and try to recruit you for them.

Becoming an Expert Game Player

Here's the overall Game plan of this book.

First, we learn to *detect* Games. By naming the Games we put the spotlight of awareness on them. This allows us to flush out the sick and morbid Games that have terrible payoffs and empowers us to refuse them. Game detection means becoming mindful, aware, conscious. It's the wake up call. It's like the wake up call that Neo received in the movie, *The Matrix*. Until he took the red pill and woke up to the Matrix that he had been living in, he didn't even know what Game he had been playing, or rather, what Game had been playing him!

Second, we *access the personal power* it takes to play the Games. It takes energy, power, and vitality to become conscious, to look the Games in the face and to decide which ones to give thumbs up and which ones to give thumbs down.

Third, we access the higher frames of our mind to turn on even greater sources of power and insight. This introduces the human dynamic of *frames* into the picture and underscore the cognitive-behavioral nature of our lives. As we think and believe, so we play the Games that we do. Games are governed and directed by frames. This provides us the central leverage point regarding how to transform things quickly. It doesn't take years of analysis. It takes the change of a frame. We use two raw and primordial powers to do that—our powers to confirm and to disconfirm, to say "Yes" and "No." By these powers we exercise executive control regarding which Games we'll play and which we will no longer tolerate.

Fourth, we will *temper this power* lest it goes to our heads. We will qualify our frames with the kinds of frames that will texture our Games so that we play the Slimming Games with the kind of values, visions, and beliefs that truly keep us balanced, healthy, and sane.

Fifth, we will learn a *structural template* so that we can quickly or extensively analyze games. Frame analysis will enable us to become more strategic and thoughtful in our approach. It will enable us to not be blind-sided by facets of our Games that we didn't see.

Sixth, after that we will explore the world of *the Slimming Games*. This is Part III where recommended slimming and fitness Games are introduced for your success in weight management. These are the Games that allow you to take charge of your world, your responses, your body, your health and fitness, and your ability to make a difference. Here you'll get to decide which Games to say "No" to and which ones to validate with a "Yes! Let's Play!"

Last, in the area of eating and exercising in ways that support being slim and fit, as in most other complex domains of life, there will be Games for different seasons. Game for becoming aware of Food Games (Ch. 7), Games that are sick and Games for rejecting the Sick Games (Ch. 8 and 4), Games for eating in an appropriate and satisfying way (Ch. 10 and 11), Games for exercising in a way that creates vitality (ch. 12), Games for sustaining your achievements (Ch. 13).

Ready to Play?

If you're ready to have at it, then I'd recommend you read the book in its entirety to get a sense of the overall Game plan. Then return a second time with a Game Plan Notebook and the ability to play the Implementation Game. Then you can pick and choose the Slim and Fit Games that you want to make *yours*.

PART I:

THE WORLD OF FRAME GAMES

Chapter 1
What is a Frame Game?

Chapter 2
Frames: The Driving Force

Chapter 3
How to Play and Master Frame Games

Chapter 1

WHAT IN THE WORLD IS A "FRAME GAME?"

Welcome to the Wild and Wonderful World of Games

Every day we get up and play various *Games*. Whether we get up and get ready for work, or for the weekend, or for a vacation, we get up in some *frame of mind* about getting up and about engaging in whatever we do that day. Given such frames, we then engage in playing Games.

We do this with eating and exercising, with regard to food and movement. I wonder *what Games* you play? I wonder if you *like* the Games that you've learned to play? I wonder if you get the payoffs from those Games that you really want?

Eating ... Through the Eyes of a "Game"

I'm sure you realize that I am not using "Game" in a literal or actual sense. I'm speaking metaphorically when I describe the *actions and transactions* that we engage in with ourselves and others as "Games." If we viewed our everyday actions and transactions with others as a *"Game,"* as set of moves and plays, what Games do we play, for what outcome or payoff, how do we score, who are we playing with or against?

The Games that you play with regard to Food, Eating, Dieting, Exercising, etc. do not have to be conscious Games. Consciousness is *not* required for such play. We can carry on (and do) without much awareness about what we're actually doing.   It's amazing, but nevertheless true. We can get into habitual ways of acting, thinking, talking, and feeling and really *not* notice the "Game" in play, how it affects others, or even how it affects us... at least not in the short-run. If we step back, take a breath and think about it with a larger vision of years, then we would probably "catch the Game in play."

To get a clear view of the Games we play with food, eating, and exercising, just step back a moment from your everyday experiences with how you manage, or fail to manage, your weight and body shape. I want you to do something very special. For just a moment, I would like to invite you to view your relationship with food and activity through the eyes of *"a Game."*   Will you play this Game with me? I promise it will not hurt, and in fact, it might just begin a rejuvenating process that will enrich your life and make you wealthier in mind and body. Ready? Then here goes. Get your *Slim & Fit Notebook,* or a tape recorder, and simply respond to the following questions. There's no need to censor your responses. Just let it flow. Say or write whatever comes to mind. Since there's really no need to consciously think about your answer, respond as quickly as possible.

- *If* you viewed the activities, interactions with others, the roles, persona, etc. that you engage in, *what Games* do you play?
- What Games do the others in your life play? Name some of their Games.
- If you're over-weight, what Games have you been playing that have contributed to that? If you're under-weight and you disorder your eating by avoiding food and other things, what Games have you been playing?
- Which Games do you find really fun and enjoyable?
- Which Games bring out your best?
- Which Games do you experience as really sick or stupid?

Food *Games*

If by *"Game"* we refer to the sets of actions and interactions that occur with regard to food, then what Games have we learned best? Do you *play* any of these Games?

- "I have to Clean my Plate" Game?
- "Eat to Feel Loved and Valued" Game?
- "Food for Reward" Game?
- Have you ever played the "Eat for Anxiety" Game when you messed up or felt bad?
- Or perhaps you've played the [take deep sigh] "I just gain weight looking at food!" Game?

A *Game* not only refers to talking and acting, but can also refer to a way of thinking, a style of feeling, a pattern for communicating, along with the roles and rituals that we engage in.   At the macro-level of behavior, *a Game* refers to any of the actions and behaviors that you could pick up on a video-recorder. If we asked, "How do you actually play that Game?" then a video-recorder would provide the sensory referents. We would *see* the Game, we could *hear* the Game, we could sense the *movements* of the Game.

Watch someone play *The Blame Game* about overeating. Watch the ole index finger come out and shake it furiously in the air at someone else, present or long gone. Hear the vocal chords become tight and the volume of the person's words increase in loudness. Observe the facial expressions, the breathing patterns, the jarring movements. You can actually *see and hear* the Game. "If it weren't for the way I was raised, I wouldn't be like this."

Games give cues and clues.

In Chess, we see a particular kind of board set out on a table and two chairs facing the table. That gives us some of the first clues about the Game. If we then see someone open a small box with black and red checkers, however, we would probably shift our thinking, "They are not going to play Chess, it's a Checkers Game they are going to play." If they then begin making the "right" kind of moves with the Checkers on that board, our guess would be confirmed. If they used the Checkers as if they were Chess pieces, or in some other way that would seem foreign and unfamiliar, we would wonder, "What in the world are they doing? They're *not* playing Checkers. I don't know what they think they're doing, but I know that they're aren't playing Checkers!"

In a similar way, the Games we play in life, in business, in relationships, and with food also have cues and clues. They have rules and procedures. There is a *structure* to the way we interact, the moves we make.

When a parent or boss begins by saying, "You didn't do this right..." and has his or her index finger pointing at you, you can pretty well bet that someone is pretty close to stepping up to playing a round of *The Blame Game*. At least those initial cues would suggest such.

If, however, the words and actions that next occur go, "... and what I really should have told you was X, then I would have communicated more clearly..." we shift our thinking. "Maybe the boss is *not* going to play the Blame Game, but maybe he's setting up another kind of Game to play. Perhaps, the Solution Game. Perhaps he wants to play, *'Let's collaborate on solving this situation.'* Or perhaps, the Mutual Responsibility Game: *'I accept and assume partial responsibility for this.'*"

Mind Games

We not only play *external Games* that a video-camera could pick up in sensory based terms (terms that you can see, hear, and feel), we also play *internal Games—head Games*. We play what we commonly refer to as "Mind Games."

In this, *Games* can also refer to our way of thinking and our pattern of perceiving. For example, the confirmed pessimist knows how to regularly and consistently play the Game of looking at the world or any particular part of it *in terms of how things will go wrong, mess up, and make us feel bad*. And if they have that Game really down pat, they will play it regularly, methodically, and persistently. When we point out their Game, they will "Ain't it awful" with us.

This means that we can view what we *do* inside our heads in information processing, constructing maps to conceptualize and construct ideas, as "Games." These are *the mental Games* that we play. They only differ in that we don't actually need another person to play those Games, we can play them by ourselves.

That's the kind of Games we play *on our way to work*. As we get up in the morning, get ourselves ready, and get to work or school or whatever, we run various *patterns of thinking, imagining, feeling, anticipating, etc.* in our heads. We do the same when it comes to meal time, shopping, going out for dinner, etc. What Games do you play in your head as you set down to eat?

"Oh, God, another day of eating in an out-of-control way!" (Utter with lots of sighs)

"Oh, what a Glorious Morning, Oh, What a Glorious Day! I eat for fuel and not for emotions!" (Sing to the tune of *Oklahoma!*)

"I wish I could find a diet that would really work." (The Wishing Game)

"I have tried so hard, but nothing ever really works."

"Great, I wonder what small piece I'll learn today that will refine my skills at eating and exercising right?"

As you'll discover in the following chapters, we not only play conversation Games, action Games, mind Games, we also play Games at various *levels.* We play Games *about* our Games.

"Let's Pretend we don't Play Games" Game

"I hate the Games that I play" Game

"I Love my Games, I wouldn't part with them for the world" Game

"I know I shouldn't eat so much, but I hate to restrict myself. That feels like I'm depriving myself and losing control."

"I don't understand my weight problem. I don't eat that much."

There's a very special mechanism in our minds that explains this facet of Games. Do you know what it is?

It is the fact that we do not merely think and feel at one level of awareness, but at multiple levels. After we engage in a *mental Game* of some sort, we then experience thoughts and feelings *about* that. Doing so shifts us up to a higher logical level. Technically this takes us to the higher cognitive level that we call "meta-cognition." It's kind of like the Boss of the first Thought. This means that we have layered a level of awareness *about* our awareness. And when we do that, we move to a higher Game, a Game about a Game.

In a way, it's like *the levels within a business.* At the primary level we have people who actually create products, perform services, and engage customers. Then we have a higher level in the organization, the men and women who manage the front-line people. After that we move up higher and have another higher level of people who manage the managers, their supervisors, and so on until we move all the way up to the CEO who performs a very different kind of work than the front-line person.

A similar kind of "hierarchy" operates in our minds-and-bodies. We have levels governing and directing levels. And, as you will discover, *the power* for making changes resides at the higher levels. This explains why the highest personal empowerment, competence, efficacy, and authority involves learning to access and run that level of mind. In a nutshell, that's what this book is all about. But more about that in the next couple of chapters when we introduce the *Levels of Mind* model (called *Meta-States*). That model will provide the only theoretical understandings you'll need to navigate *the Frame Games* that you play with regard to eating and exercising.

So, in these ways, the *Games* that we play make up the very fabric of our lives. And if they make up the fabric of our subjective reality, then they control the quality of our lives, the quality of our mind and skills, the effectiveness of our actions, and so much more.

And Then There are the Frames

By *"frame,"* we refer to the most basic process of human consciousness, namely, a *frame-of-reference.* Your "frame" identifies first of all that to which you refer. Without knowing what a person is referring to, we can't communicate effectively. This explains why we so frequently ask each other when we're not "getting it," "What are you talking about?"

To talk or think, we have some *reference* in mind. These references govern the Games that we play. This is where *the levels of mind* come in. That's because we can so easily use an actual reference as our *mental reference structure.*

[As an aside, I'm using noun-like terms, "frames," "frames of reference," etc., yet these are actually *processes.* It describes *how* we are mentally *framing* or *punctuating* our experiences.]

Imagine that we eat something that messes up our diet or that we know is wrong for our bodies, or that creates a mess in some way.

Suppose we know that this mistake is going to cost us in terms of the time and effort to recover our momentum or way of life. Suppose further that some friend or loved one loses it and comes down on you with some strong words, anger, and accusation. That gives us a *reference.*

Commonly, as we see, hear, and feel the results of this "wrong," we will probably experience a state of fear, apprehension, concern, stress, upsetness, or some other negative emotion. Suppose we then *use* that reference experience as our *way of thinking* about eating in general, dieting, taking a risk in changing our habits, investing the time and trouble to learn healthy habits, etc.? To do that means that we have now just graduated to a higher level. Now the reference experience we began with, which once was an actual historical happening, has now become a *mental reference point in our brain.* Now we have shifted to using it as a template or as a frame of mind.

That's what we do with external references (which we call "experiences"). We use our life experiences to create our maps about the world. We take our experiences and draw certain conclusions from them. We make generalizations from the events about the events, about the people involved, about ourselves, etc. We *mine* the events for the *meanings* that we think lie inside the event as we mine gold, silver, lead, copper from the earth. Yet this is precisely where we all go wrong.

Why?

Because "meaning" does *not* exist *in* events and experiences. As you will shortly discover, it cannot exist there. "Meaning" is predominantly a thing of the mind... a function of our entire nervous system and brain. We *create* meaning. We *invent* it. It only occurs in the "mind" of a meaning-maker. It emerges in the process of creating connections and mental contexts. In communicating with another, we often seek to *find* and *discover* another person's "meaning." Yet that's fairly difficult to do. To discover another's meanings we have to listen apart from our mental filters, intensive listening, reflecting back what we think we've heard, and continually correct our impressions.

Because we internalize our experiences and use them as *reference points*, we build up a system of "meanings" and then *see the world in terms of those meaning frames.* Eventually we develop layers of nested frames within frames, meanings inside of meanings. Then we take our *frame of mind,* add lots of repetition it habituates, and so it becomes our way of thinking, our cognitive *framework.* It is this entire *framework* of nested frames that govern what and how we understand, think, perceive, reason, believe, etc. It forms and structures what we call "personality" and our "neuro-semantic" states. We then carry that reference system with us everywhere we go. We use it to play various Games. Depending on the meanings that we've made, our *frames of mind* prepare us for specific Games.

- "Never Take a Chance. Play it Safe" Game
- "What if they laugh at you?" Game
- "Making Mistakes is Terrible" Game, "Therefore always cover your butt."
- "Fat is a genetic thing; I can't make any difference in my weight, fitness, or health" Game.
- "It's just calories anyway" Game.
- "If only I could find an easy program" Game
- "I've tried and it just doesn't make much difference" Game
- "It's never going to work!" Game
- "But what about my immediate gratification?" Game

Frames describe the content and structure of our thoughts and set us up for the Games we are permitted to play, know how to play, and want to play. Within the term *frame* we include all of the higher level cognitive structures. This includes all those mental phenomena that we commonly call beliefs, values, understandings, paradigms, mental models, expectations, assumptions, decisions, identifications, etc.

Together we have "Frame Games"

Putting *Games* and *Frames* together gives us **Frame Games.** This describes both the internal and external facets of our experiences, and so the full range of mental and behavioral Games that govern and to a great extent define the life that we live. In eating and exercising, like work, personal life, health, wealth building, learning, etc., we all play out various Frame Games in how we live our lives. By our *frames* we establish the Games, both the good ones and the destructive ones. Our

Games imply and flow from the governing frames.

With this introduction, we can now look at some of the not-so desirable *Frame Games* that go on in the arena of the two habits that mostly affect our weight and general physical fitness—eating and exercising. The mere fact that *Games* go on in these domains is not particularly insightful. Most of us already know that. That information alone isn't all that helpful. However, that the Games we play operate as functions of our frames, is insightful and useful.

How?

Awareness of the frames gives us insight into where the Games come from, what endows them with *meaning*, motivation, and power. And, knowing that then gives us some choices with regard to what we want to do about it. Conversely, when we lack awareness of either the Game, the frame, or the governing influence of the frame, we then can so easily get caught up in the Game. When that happens, then *the Frame Game plays us,* rather than us playing the Frame Games that we design and choose.

- What Games are currently *playing* you regarding food and exercise?
- Are you consciously choosing to play those Games?
- Do those Games support you and move you in the kind of direction that you want for yourself, the kind of vitality and body shape?
- What Game or Games would you prefer to be playing?
- What cues and triggers hook you into the Games?
- What frames drive these Games?
- What do you believe about these Games?
- What historical or conceptual references do you use to generate the frame?
- How long have you been stuck in certain frames?

Indicators of Unhealthy and Destructive Games

I have already enumerated some of the not-so fun Games that sometimes we find ourselves playing with food. These reduce the quality of life and when unchecked can induce a sense of meaninglessness and futility. Did some of them particularly speak to you? Here's another quick check-list of Games. Check those that you find yourself involved in that do not enhance your fitness, energy level, or sense of self-confidence. Identify those that undermine you and your success. And because this only represents a small sample of potential Games, take a few moments to identify other not-so useful Games that are playing you.

    Unenhancing Frame Games:

The Helpless Game	You Can't Really Change Anything. I'm a Victim of my genetics, family, upbringing, etc. I'm Powerless to Change my weight, my eating habits, my exercising habits, etc.
Peevishness Game:	I shouldn't have to do all this work in order to be thin. It's unfair.
Paranoid Game:	The doctors, diet programs, media, etc. are out to get me, to sucker me into the latest fad.
The Blame Game	If it weren't for my mother (father, teachers, husband, etc.) Game If it weren't for the commercials, for the restaurants making the food so appealing.
Over-Responsible Game:	I'm responsible for everything, that's why I eat as I do. I have to de-stress. I feel so responsible for the messes that others get into and then need to eat to calm myself.
Stress Game:	I can't feel a sense of relief or comfort without some food. There's too much to do, I can't juggle everything.

Sorting for Games

    If you have ever communicated with a friend or loved one about taking charge of your weight, going to Weight Watchers, or thinking about cutting out a lot of the fat in your diet, and then felt the lack of support from them, then you experienced someone playing a Game with you. It's as if you come together, each have a different Game in mind to play, and yet both fail to notice. Both assumed that the other was ready to play. Then came the mis-matching of the transactions. The moves seemed only to underscore that you are not on the same page, not playing the same Game.

Now suppose you began to wonder about what *frame* that other person must have in his or her head that creates this mismatch.

"There she's goes again, talk, talk, talk. It will go nowhere."

"People should accept their weight and stop trying to better themselves; it's really vanity."

"Diets and programs don't work."

Given this way of thinking, the behavior of the loved one or friend now makes perfect sense. In fact, we can say that that person *has to* act and talk that way. *Given that frame*, the person has no choice about what Game to play. That person does not "see" things as you do. That person does not "get it" from your perspective.

That so many people *try* to do something about their energy level and weight, but never succeed indicates that we commonly play some very ineffective, useless, and even destructive Games. We may have to deal with those toxic, morbid, and unuseful Games before we commission ourselves to play some new Game. The helpless whiny victim Game is especially toxic for undermining success. So is the, *"Hey, I can't help it; I'm not responsible for my weight"* Game. Such non-enhancing frames invite and initiate other non-enhancing Frame Games.

What non-enhancing Games are you currently experiencing and playing? To check this out simply begin by noting your *state of mind* about food, self-control, healthy habits, exercise, etc.

- What do you think?
- What comes to mind?
- Do you sense that there is little to no chance of taking effective action, making a difference in how you feel and look, sustaining your new approach and making it your lifestyle?

- Do you feel enough self-respect and self-confidence to do this?
- What Games are you playing in your mind, thought-world, feelings, and behaviors?

"States" and Frame Games

There's a great way to detect the Games afoot in our lives about food. It involves examining our state or attitude. I use the term *"state"* to refer to the sum total of your mental, emotional, and behavioral experience at any given moment. Are you in an excited state? A depressed state? Would you characterize your state as stressful, angry, pleasant, playful, or what?

In any given day, we typically experience a great many states regarding the Games that we play. Some of these are appropriate and resourceful, others are inappropriate and unresourceful. When we "cop an attitude," we typically enter into a pretty unresourceful state of mind-and-body. We're not at our best. *"State"* is a great word for this because it holistically captures both the mental (cognitive) and emotional (bodily) facets of our experience.

As a leading researcher in the field of psycho-biology, Ernest Rossi (1987) has noted our *states* create *a mind-set or attitude set.* This means that once we get into a state, *the state* itself governs our learning, memory, perception, communication, and behavior. He calls this *state-dependency.*

For example, once in an angry state, we tend to perceive the world in terms of hostility. Our learning and memory does service to the anger. So do our actions and communications. So with every intense state (joy, playfulness, relaxation, tension, fear, etc.), once in the state, the state controls the rest of our psychological powers.

Imagine sprinting at full speed in a race on a track. How likely will it be that you will be thinking and feeling depressive thoughts at that moment? In fact, almost regardless of your thinking before or after, both your mind-set and the chemical processes required for depression will not be available while you are running. The experience of running (as with every experience) holistically involves mind-and-body. So even when you begin to think about running a race, you might very well start to change your state and even begin to feel different.

What does this mean in terms of the Games that we play around eating and exercising? It means that our *state,* at any given moment, sets the physical and emotional background (and frames) for the Games we play and determines the quality of our Games.

- What state would you have to experience in order to blame?
- What state would you have to access in order to seek solutions in a positive way?
- What state would support you in problem solving?
- What state would support you to feel de-motivated, fearful, or over-controlling?

Motivated States and Frame Games

When we think about mastering our weight, especially developing an expertise *at effectively handling our eating and exercising habits,* the subject of *motivation* inevitably comes up. In the area of food, the whole question of what motivates, how to motivate, external and/or internal motivators, etc. describes an immense and critically important area. *Frame Games* gives us a particularly helpful way to think about this.

- What Games do you play regarding food, "dieting," and exercise when it comes to "motivation?"
- Do you wake up in the morning full of excitement and passion about your own self-management or control?
- Do you wake up and groan and moan and play the, "Why do I have to watch my eating" Game?

Whether you play the Game of loving or hating the opportunity to discover and implement new habits that support eating and exercising in a healthy way, you have some frame and frames-of-frames that govern and support those Games. In this, they both create the state and reflect the state.

Does it surprise you to realize that wanting to take action towards your goals and *not* wanting to take action both involve the same process—a process of setting a frame and then actualizing that frame. In both cases, we use our consistent focus on our goal to follow through.

We move toward making something happen or we move toward making something *not* happen.

How is it that sometimes a person brand new to a field with little or no experience will enter into it and tremendously succeed? How is it that some people will consistently just go for their dreams and make them happen, while others, who may be far more informed and talented, find themselves crippled by hesitation?

The answer is this: It's all a matter of frames.

Some people play the frame Game of "Focusing on My Goals and making them Happen." Others play the Frame Game of "I sure don't want to get any failures today. I've had enough of that."

Summary

- There are Games abroad in the domain of eating and exercising that radically and profoundly affect what and how we handle these facets of everyday life. We play Games in how we eat, why we eat, what we seek to accomplish in eating, etc. We also play mental Games with ourselves and others as we engage ourselves with food, with exercising, etc.

- Behind (or above) every Game there is a Frame. Frames drive Games. To play a Game, we have to learn the rules, the structure, the payoffs, etc.

- *Frame Games* gives us a new way to think about the sets of interactions on the behavioral, communicational, and psychological levels for analyzing, understanding, and effectively working with the Games that aren't enhancing.

- As there are a lot of sick, toxic, and morbid Games that can make us unsane, so there are a lot of enhancing, empowering, and fun Games that make for an increased sense of sanity and enable us to become highly productive.

- If we want to become *experts* in handling the processes of eating and exercising and developing the expertise and quality of *excellence* in this area, we only need to know how to stop playing the foolish and destructive Games, and how to play the ones that bring out our best.

Now That You Know—Here's What To Do

- Make a list of your Food Games. Just watch yourself as you move through the next week and *Name the Game*. What Games do you play with Food? Give them a funny memorable name.
- Appoint someone in your life to play *Naming the Food Game* with you. Have fun.

ALL OF LIFE IS A GAME PLAYED OUT INSIDE OF SOME FRAME.

WHEN YOU KNOW THAT, IT'S ONLY A QUESTION OF WHAT GAMES ARE YOU PLAYING AND WHAT FRAMES SET UP THOSE GAMES.

WHAT ARE THE RULES OF THE GAMES?
WHEN DO YOU START?
WHEN DO YOU QUIT?

HOW DO YOU SCORE POINTS?
HOW DO
YOU WIN?
WHAT ARE THE PAYOFFS?

DOES THE GAME ENHANCE YOUR LIFE?
DOES IT EMPOWER YOU AS A PERSON?

Chapter 2

FRAMES:
THE DRIVING FORCE
IN THE
FIT AND SLIM GAME

Where there's a Game,
There's a Frame
(Frame Game Secret, *Frame Games)*

It's inescapable that you show up at every meal and every snack in some *frame of mind.* We're always in some *state* or *frame* of mind and body; in fact, we never leave home without our frames. These invisible mental and emotional states govern our everyday experiences as *the hidden driving or animating force* behind our lives. As such, they also animate all of our experiences with regard to eating and exercising. Given that, let's begin by asking some questions to raise our *frame* awareness:

- What *frame of mind* do you show up with regarding eating and exercising?
- What *frame of mind* do you have about *that* frame of mind?
- How well does your mental frame serve you in terms of health, fitness, staying slim and trim, etc.?
- Do you find your emotional frame of mind empowering?

The terms "frame" and "frame of mind" have become pretty common terms. They are phrases that we typically use in everyday life.

Additionally, there are some common synonyms that we also use a lot when talking about our frames. We commonly talk about our frames in terms of our "attitude" or even "mood." And as we all know, *attitude is everything.*

It's All About Frames

When we're involved in a Game, it seems to be all about our actions and emotions and all about the actions and emotions that we receive from others. This seems especially true of those Games that we do not like. At those times, it seems to be all about the Game. Yet it is not.

When someone is pointing a finger at you and blaming, it seems like it's all about the Blame Game. When someone's is intimidating, manipulating, ordering your around, playing you off of someone else, running a scam, complaining, bellyaching, etc., *inside* of such Games, it certainly seems like the immediate talk, actions, feelings, and consequences are everything. "That's all it is!" we say. But that's deceptive.

A Game is only the Game that it is
because of some Frame.

"Checkers" is only the experience and set of interactions that we call "Checkers" when there's are two players and they are playing by the rules in their heads about how "Checkers" ought to be played. This highlights *the structure* within, behind, or above the Game or what I am calling, the Frame.

Consider the Game of Criticism. I used to criticize freely and so became quite skilled at it! Any time I saw something amiss from what *I* thought ought not to be, I critiqued it I did so in order to make things better.

Of course, I didn't find many who really wanted to play that Game with me and be the receiver. I would start in at various times and places and offer my insightful critiques and lo, and behold, they didn't seem to want to play! Or if they did, they wanted to change roles and be the giver of the critique. Strange.

Now come to think of it, I didn't act much like an enthusiastic partner when people wanted to play the Game with me either. "You need to..." "You should..." "Have you ever thought of ...?" They'd initiate the game of "Let's Criticize What You're Doing Wrong" Game and somehow it just didn't feel like a version of, "I Want to Help You Make Your Life Wonderful!" Game

I have no doubt that one of my highest *frames,* and one of their highest *frames,* in criticism was to make things better. Yet there were some other frames involved.

For the One Trying to Play the Game:
    I don't like what's going on and I'm going to let you know.
    I feel upset, angry, frustrated, etc. and you're the cause.
    I think you're Wrong and I'm going to set you Straight.
    I wouldn't have done it that way; so you shouldn't?
    What's wrong with you, are you stupid?
For the Reluctant One Who Doesn't Want to Play that Game:
    I hate being reproved, corrected, straightened out.
    Who gave *You* the right to criticize me?
    I'm in no mood to take this from you!
    Shut up! I don't want to know about my failings or fallibilities.

Of course, with those Frames, no wonder "criticism" seldom works to make things better. No wonder both person criticizing, and person receiving the communication, do not use the Game for improving things, gaining deeper understandings, or feeling honored to be so engaged with each other. No wonder the Game of Criticism more typically ends up being a Push-Shove Game.

    You ought to... No, You're Wrong, I ought not to do that! ... Well, then you are just stupid about these matters! . ... Who are you calling Stupid? ... I'm calling you stupid...

Understanding the Power of Frames

A *frame of reference* governs our thinking, emoting, speaking, and responding because it sets a context for how we view and interpret things. It establishes a conceptual context that governs the meanings we use and create in our responses. Without a frame, a Game has no meaning, no rules, no winners or losers, no time limits or any other kind of limits. The power that governs the quality of our actions, skills, and even life lies in our *frames.* So as we say with someone who has a powerfully positive attitude or who "cops an attitude" in a negative and hurtful way, *attitude is everything.*

Frames create meaning. I mentioned earlier that "meaning" as a crucial human phenomenon does not, and cannot exist in an external event or experience. Let me further highlight this by saying that *meaning itself is not "real."* It is not "real" in any external way. That's why you never walk out of your house in the morning, or office at noon, and stumble over a hunk of meaning.

"Hey, who left this hunk of meaning in the driveway?"

"Meaning" is not that kind of a thing. It's not a "thing" at all. It's a way of conceptualizing things. It's a *way of thinking* that we *hold* in mind (hence the original significance of "meaning," "to hold in mind"). This process nature of meaning makes it slippery, plastic, and difficult to manage. And yet meaning (what we hold in mind as significant) is what gives our lives significance and power. Meaning drives and motivates. Meaning governs what we can sell and what we cannot sell. It's meaning that brings out our best and enables us to reach into the depths and heights of our hearts and mind and become *experts at managing our weight,* or fail to do so.

If meaning plays that much of a role in our lives, in the expression of our actions and behaviors, in our communications and feelings, in the quality of our lives, then let's explore what we mean by *meaning.*

- What does anything "mean?"
- What does your food or exercise mean to you?
- What meanings do you give to succeeding or achieving a particular goal that you've set for yourself?
- What meanings really turn you on?
- What meanings do you really believe in and invest yourself into?
- What's so meaningful about those meanings?
- What doesn't mean that much to you?

In asking these "meaning" questions, we are asking about your *frame of references at many levels*, we are asking about your *frame of mind* at many levels, and we are asking about such frames as—

- Belief Frames
- Value Frames

- Destiny Frames
- Identity Frames
- Expectation Frames
- Outcome Frames
- Emotional Frames
- Theological Frames
- Philosophical Frames

It's Frames All the Way Up

"Mind" has levels. That's because we never just think, we are a class of life that has the most amazing ability to *think about our thinking.* Technically we call this "self-reflexive consciousness." Upon thinking about what went on at work on Monday (first level thinking), we can then think about *the quality or nature of our thinking.* We can step back, so to speak, and reflect on ourselves—our thoughts, our feelings, our experiences, our history, future, ideas, etc. We call this recursive nature of thinking meta-cognition. The term *"meta"* here refers to a higher level that is *above* something else:

A thought *about* another thought:
What's the quality of my thinking?
A feeling *about* another feeling:
I'm *afraid* that my *confidence* in that task isn't strong enough.
A thought *about* a feeling:
I wonder if that is an appropriate fear or just a worry?
A feeling *about* a thought:
I feel so stressed out when I think about the way he communicates.
A feeling about a thought about a feeling:
I worry that my decision to eat and exercise more healthily will confirm my fears that it won't work.

As a symbolic class of life, our ability to denote a word, idea, feeling, experience, event, etc. with a word or a symbol enables us to move up the levels of awareness. This creates our ability to think conceptually, to abstract to more complex understandings of things, to create our sciences, philosophies, and higher psychological states of mind. It's a great power. It's also a terrible power when misused or abused. When we do not handle it well or when we abuse it, we create living hells of closed-ended spirals that only take us into more confusion and limitation (see *Dragon Slaying,* 2000).

Like the hierarchy of a corporate business, *the higher frames govern personality or consciousness* as a boss or CEO governs a corporation. In any living system of interactive parts, the higher levels organize, modulate, and control the processes of the entire system. The boss, CEO, board of directors, or someone at the top creates the policies, sets the rules, establishes the operational directives, etc.

What you think about food is important. Yet what you think and frame about those food ideas and feelings are even more important. At the first level, "Food is valuable and tasty" isn't all that critical of an idea. It doesn't create a particularly toxic Game. But when you think, "The value and tastiness of food is what gives me a feeling of being full and rewarded, 'the good life.'" now that might just set you up to over-value it and to play the *Food is Personal Reward and Validation* Game.

In a similar way, our higher frames govern our thinking, feeling, speaking, acting, relating, development and use of skills, etc. Our higher frames establish the existence of certain Games, the rules that we play by, the limits we recognize or refuse to recognize, who can play, etc. The Games we play with regard to our jobs and careers, our motivation and commitment, our relationships and self-discipline, etc. are all derived from our *frames of mind*.

The Roadblock of Howard's Frame of Mind

One of the first persons I worked with on weight loss was Howard. More than a client, he was a good friend and wanted help with getting into shape and taking control of his eating habits. Knowing Howard, I knew that they were atrocious. It wasn't long before I hit a roadblock in his mental attitude.

"You just don't understand, I've tried and I just can't stop myself from eating in all the wrong ways."

"What do you mean you can't stop yourself?"

"Well, I can start with the best of intentions, but when I'm at church potlucks or at an all-you-can-eat buffet, I forget and I end up eating far too much ... and I eat the wrong foods. I eat foods fried in heavy oils, and the deserts loaded with sugar; I just can't help myself."

"An alien force takes over your arm and forces the food down your throat. Is that what happens?"

[Laughing] "No, no. I just forget about losing weight. All I can think about is how good the roast will taste, the mashed potatoes and gravy, the pork chops... [licking his lips]... I just get into a different state of mind and think that a little more won't hurt."

"So, Howard, that's the Game you play?"

"Game? What Game?"

"The 'A little more won't hurt!' Game. You think that way and you really feel that way. You look at your plate and think, 'That little bit more is nothing!' That's the Game you play with Food, isn't it?."

"Well, I don't think of it that way."

"Then how do you think of it?"

"It's just that a bite is nothing... that it won't make cause me to weight any more or that if I didn't eat it, that I'd weigh any less."

"Ah, another Game!"

"What?"

"You also play the Game of 'My eating habits and style does not really affect my weight gain or loss.' 'Taking this or that particular bite can't make all that much of a difference.' Now that's quite a Game! You can discount any and probably all of your eating behavior because you keep it so particularized, that you *discount* it's overall significance.' That's quiet a skill!"

"But it doesn't. One more bite at any meal can't ..."

"Playing the Game with me, huh? Want me to buy into that Game, do you?"

"No, it's just that..."

"Ah, the Game is fighting for itself. Fighting to justify itself. Do you hear it, Howard? Do you really want to play this Game?"

That interrupted him a bit, that's when I invited him to quality control his Games.

Quality Controlling our Frames & Frame Games

Given this, as soon as we recognize and detect our Games and Frames, shouldn't we *quality control* our frames and Games? We *quality control* by checking out our Frame Games to make sure that they support and contribute to our goals. Shouldn't we make sure that we're playing healthy and life-enhancing games? And how do we do that?

- How healthy are the *games* Ghat you play with food?
- Do the Games enrich your skills, relationships, development, etc.?
- Do you have any *frames of mind* that get in your way and undermine your ability to achieve?
- What *Frame Games* limit or hinder you?
- Which ones support, empower, enrich, and bring out your best?
- What *Frame Games* enable you to play the scenario of health and weight control?
- Do any of them seduce you into playing the Fat Game?
- Do you need that Game?

These are some of the questions I asked Howard. As I did, it soon become crystal clear to him that he did not need to so frame food. The Games that he was playing in his head and body around food were undermining his personal effectiveness and health. He was ready to say, "Hell, No! I don't need to play it this way anymore!"

As the Total Quality Movement raised awareness in the work place about the role and value of *quality,* so this technique of quality controlling the content of our thoughts gives us a *human technology* for bringing *quality* to our brain and to our Games. In business, we have learned that *quality* sells, it makes money, it creates long-term business and enduring relationships, etc. It similarly enriches our personal lives.

Quality thinking and feeling at the personal level has a whole list of similar benefits in terms of the habits we establish around food and activity. When we make sure that the Games we play with ourselves and others are *quality Games*, it supports our long term success. It makes our relationship to food and exercise fun. This reduces the stress and tension that arises when we forget to be human. The new Games are not about dieting at all, they are about *how* we live.

Here's another great thing about all of this. When we learn how to play *Quality Games*—others will want to play with us. This creates quality relationships that not only support our health, vitality, energy, fitness, etc., but enables us to enjoy ourselves and become more of who we can become along the way. This contributes to keeping us balanced and healthy.

Frames for Changing Games

If frames operate as *the driving force* within the Games that we play, then when we change a frame, *we alter a Game.* Transforming our frames of mind (or attitudes) can involve many different transformations. We could change the rules of the Game, the name of the Game, the conditions and situations for the Game, the players, the way we score, how we value the Game, what we believe about the Game, etc. Sometimes the tiniest change in the frame alters the Game in an irrevocable way. At other times, a frame change will refine, hone, and heighten a Game— make it more sane, humane, compassionate, fun.

We call a change or alteration in a frame, *a reframe.* In the place of one reference point, we substitute another. "Eating is about fuel, not being rewarded." This could involve a change of perspective, another set of criteria, or a transformation in the structure of the frame. "I eat to live, I do not live to eat." Reframing, as a mental shift, invites us try on new perspectives. Reframing operates as *a driving force* that can renew, rejuvenate, and refresh the Game that we play.

Frames for Being Fit and Slim

Throughout this book I focus on *a healthy and balanced fitness, and weight management.*

Excellence in any field involves finding and replicating the strategies of those who show the highest expertise in that area. At the surface level of things, this directs our focus to *the content of what* the expert does that defines him or her as an "expert." What are the necessary skills, activities, understandings, etc.?

Yet excellence involves more. Much more. It involves *attitude.* What are the beliefs, ideas, and attitudes that support the expert in attaining, sustaining, and demonstrating high level performances? What is the expert's attitude about the boring details involved in mastery? What attitude does the expert take about any given facet of eating or exercising? How does the expert think or feel when failure, rejection, frustration, etc. occur?

Such questions as these enables us to look at not only the external factors that contribute to excellence, but the internal and psychological factors of success. In terms of the model here,

- What are the mental Games that experts play that set them head and shoulders above the rest of the crowd?
- What are the verbal and linguistic Games that they play that enable them to control their states and stay fresh and creative?
- What are the behavioral Games that they play?
- How do they frame things about X or Y which enhances and supports their persistence?

Summary

- There is a *structure to excellence* and within that structure, the driving force for expertise in any field involves the higher frames of mind that governs the person's internal world.
- A Game is only the Game it is because of the *frame* that drives it. This makes Frame Game detection critical for accessing weight mastery.
- It's frames all the way up because we are a special class of life—a class that lives and thrives on symbols, and especially language. We frame, and we frame our frames.

Now That You Know—Here's What To Do

- Use your *Game Notebook* and identify some of the Frames of References and Frames of Mind that set up the Food Games that you have been playing. What are the Rules of the Games?
- Which of these mental Frames are obviously useless even stupid that will be easy to say "No" to? Which Frames seem to make some sense?

THE NAME OF THE GAME
IS TO NAME THE GAME

What Games have you been Playing with Food?

What Games do you need to Quit Playing?

What Games would you prefer to Play?

Chapter 3

HOW TO PLAY & MASTER

FRAME GAMES

An Overview of Mastering Frame Games

You will find *playing Games* easy because you already know what a Game is and how to play Games. Actually, you've been doing this all of your life, now we just want to make it conscious.

As we have noted, a *"Game"* simply refers to a set of actions and inter-actions that allow you to structure your energies so that you can achieve some desired objective. That's why we play "Games." We want to accomplish something; we want to "win" at something, express our skills, get some payoff, show off or discover our knowledge and abilities. We want to relate to someone in a certain way, and/or simply enjoy the process of living and expending our energies.

Also, as we play Games, we do so according to *the rules of the particular Game.* These rules set up the structure, form, and nature of the Games. The rules give us an understanding of when we play, who we play with, how we play, why we play, how we score, when to start, when to quit, exceptions, etc. Without the *rules* of the Game, we could not play. Without the rules, there would be chaos.

Ron talked about discovering the rules of his eating Games after reading *Games Slim People Play.*

"I really didn't like what I was finding out about myself and I did have to keep telling myself that eating is just eating and that it doesn't mean I'm bad or wrong. Funny how the mind works that way. Anyway, I realized how easily 'eating times' would seduce me. I would actually eat and even *feel* like eating simply because of the time of the clock. It was stupid. I guess I had a rule in my head, 'When it's 7 a.m., 12 noon, and 6;30 p.m.— Eat!'"

This describes how *Frame Games* work. The Games that we play arise from, and are given form by, *our frames of mind.* That's why the very first thing we need to do in learning a new Game is to clearly identify the *frames* that initiate, institute, and structure the Game. When we first learned chess, monopoly, baseball, tennis, or any game, we began by asking, "Okay, how do we play?" "How do we get started?"

We typically do not learn Games by studying the formal rule books. We learn just enough rules to begin and then we play around with the Game until we get the hang of it.

We learn Games best by trying them on and giving ourselves a chance to learn the ropes.

We also give ourselves a chance with the new Game by *not* expecting that we have to begin as experts or masters. Do you play new Games that way? If so, stop it! That will only undermine your effectiveness. It's going to take some time and lots of practice to learn and become skilled at a new Game. So lighten up. Give yourself a break. Begin by just having fun with it, learning, making mistakes, using the feed back of what works and what does not that we will learn the new Game more efficiently. Given this, here are some of my recommendations as you read about some new Games here.

1) First, get an initial impression about the Game.

Start with the name of the Game. What is it called? Often, just knowing the name of the Game is enough to get you started. This is also the value of giving Games colloquial names that are memorable. "The No-Blame, No-Shame Game," for instance, provides a nice initial impression that specifies the governing frame. Soon I will introduce the "Food for Fuel" Game and the "Psycho-Eating" Game. These names describe the Game.

2) Begin playing the Game and experimenting around with it.

We learn best and most thoroughly as we experiment, test, and play around with the Game. Take the *governing idea* and play around with it. Toss it back and forth with someone. Get a feel for it. Express it in numerous ways. Apply it to work, home, exercise, friendship, etc. Don't aim to do anything with it except just testing and playing with it. Make the Game *yours* by playing around with the ideas, rules, processes, etc. that will customize it to you.

3) Visit the description of the Game to begin filling in some of the details.

One reason most of us do *not* start a new Game by reading the rule book is that we do not want to overwhelm ourselves with all of the Game details. There is also another reason. We usually discover the meaningfulness of the rules if we learn them bit by bit, trying out what we know, testing it in experience, getting a feel for the initial structures, experiencing the contexts in which they make sense, and then returning for the next piece.

It's similar to learning to work with a computer or computer program. We start by reading a step or two, acting on those, seeing if we get them right, making sure that we are orienting ourselves to the computer or the program properly, and then adding one or two pieces at a time.

Another reason for this incremental approach is that it makes *the Game primary* rather than the rules. The rules and frames are there to support the Game, not as a substitute for the Game. A weird thing happens to a person when the rules become uppermost and the Game secondary. People who come to care more about *the rules* than the Game tend to become tyrants and poor losers. They don't *play* well.

4) Continually renew your focus and awareness on the objective of the Game.

What is the purpose of the Game? Why do you want to play this particular Game? What is the payoff that you want? That which enlivens and energizes any Game is it's sense of direction, outcome, and purpose.

In the *Frame Games* of our lives, many Games actually operate as sub-Games within yet larger Games. The purpose of one Game may therefore be to enable us to play a larger Game. Knowing this can give our playing more meaning and purpose. So look for the larger Game frames within which you're playing. When you win this particular Game, what higher Game does it allow you to play?

5) Have fun as you play.

No matter where you are in the process, whether you are a novice at a new Game or a master, don't forget to have fun and to enjoy the process. This will support your learning, development, and expertise. Remember also that most of the fun is in the play itself rather than in the Game prize; it's in the process. So keep Quality Controlling your new Games for fun:

"Am I having fun?"

"How could I do this *and* have some fun?"

6) Keep aiming for mastery by developing more skills and taking on more challenges.

In any Game there is a relationship between your skills in playing the Game and the challenge which the Game offers you. When we experience high challenges, but have a low skill level, we typically feel overwhelmed. This creates anxiety. When that happens, it reduces our fun and delight in the Game. We then begin to get serious, stressed, and often will feel inadequate. That's why we need to start off slow and easy.

And yet, not too low. When we face a Game that has low challenge and do so with low level skills, the Game hardly seems worth learning. It feels boring. It doesn't seem to matter much one way or the other. So our interest wanes. We feel no passion about the Game. We easily dismissed such Games, "So what?"

Similarly, if we have developed high level skills for a particular Game and yet face a low challenge from another player, then also we get bored. "Why bother?" The Game seems like a child's Game, there's no real call to or challenge to our skills. It's too easy. And as it becomes too easy, our interest and passion wanes.

The best situation occurs when we coordinate highly developed skills with bold challenges which call forth our highest passions. Then we not only feel drawn into the Game, compelled to play at our best, but we can then get lost in the Game. When that happens, something magical occurs—we experience what Csikszentmihalyi, a cognitive psychologist, calls "flow." When you get into this magical realm, the world goes away, time goes away, a sense of self goes away, and all of the higher levels of the mind vanish as we become totally present in the moment and fully experiencing the Frame Game.

The following chapters enumerates lots of "Games"—Frame Games that you can learn to play for greater management over yourself, your eating, weight, etc. Treat them as *Games.* Treat the *frames* as all of the rules, structures, and formatting that allows you to play the Games. As you identify the old Games that you have been playing (and their corresponding frames), and the new Games that you can play if you so choose, you move to a new position. You can now choose how and why you play the Game of life as you do.

Mastering Games Via *Frame Game Analysis*

After we learn to become a master at controlling the Games that we play, we an move up to an even higher Game to play. We can engage in the Game of Game Analysis. The following questions enable you to play this higher and nearly magical Game of *Game Analysis.* Thinking through the structure and form of the Game brings insight and clarity. And since clarity is our strength, it empowers us to take charge of the Games that we play and the frames that we allow to control our mind.

There is rhyme and reason to the Games we play. They do not occur as accidents or as mere happen-chance events. Unique and personal understandings govern our Games.

To transform your eating and exercising habits, grab your Game Notebook so that you can use it to record the Frame Games that you catch. Then you can analyze them. The following questions will lead you to more fully describe the Game. It enables you to name the Game. That's important. It's one of the *Frame Game secrets,* namely, *The Name of the Game is to Name the Game.*

By naming the Game, we gain control over it. That's the first step. As long as *the Game plays us* and we don't know it, we don't know *how* it controls us, or the structure of the Game features— we are its patsy. As you stubbornly refuse to tolerate that kind of mental and emotional slavery, you'll be able to develop true mastery over the Games that you play.

Frame Game Analysis

Frame Game Analysis blows the whistle on the Games that go nowhere as well as those that waste our time and energy. The analysis gives us the mindfulness so that we can make some really clear choices. Then we can powerfully say *"No!"* To the toxic old Games and *"Yes!"* to the empowering life Games.

What's the Game?

What's the Game that you're playing with food?
With eating?
With exercising?
With controlling your appetites?
With disciplining your responses?
With running your own brain?
With managing your own states?

Who are the Players in the Game?

Who do you play the Games with? (Just self or others?)
How many people do you invite into the Games?
Are all of the players living?

How healthy, productive, useful, enhancing, etc. is the Game?

Do you like the Games you're playing?
Do they serve you well?
Do they enhance your life?
Do they empower you as a person?
Are they useful, practical, or productive?
Would you recommend them to your children?

What are the hooks that pull you into the Games?

What starts the Game? How does it begin?

How do the Games hook you?
What's within the Games that's seductive, tempting?
What's the payoff that pulls us into the Game?
What are some of the triggers that get you?
What bait does the Game depend upon to get you?

What are some of the cues that indicate the presence of a Game?

How do you know when you're involved in playing a Game?
What lets you know?
What are some of the linguistic cues? (The way that you talk)
What are some of the physical cues? (Things that you are doing)
What are some of the environmental cues?
What begins and ends the Game?
When is it over?

What are the Rules of the Game?

How is the Game set up?
How do you play?
How do you "score" points in the Game?
What comprises a "win?"
What lets you know that you are "losing?"
Who makes up the rules?
Do you like the rules?

What would you like to call this Frame Game?

Now that you have described many of the facets of the Game, what would you like to *name* this Game so as to take control of the frame Games that you play?
What funny, silly, memorable, and colloquial name would really summarize this Frame Game?

What frames of reference support and drive this Game?

Are you using historical referents?
· Imagined referents?
Conceptual referents?

Vicarious referents (something that happened to someone else)?
Health or unhealthy referents?
Enhancing or limiting referents?

What's the Agenda of the Game?

What's the intention or motivation that drives the Game?
What payoffs do you get from the Game?
What hidden agendas outside of your awareness may be motivating the Game?

What's the Emotional Intensity of the Game?

How much intensity from 0 to 10 does the Game generate?
Are there any somatic responses that the Game produces?
Are there any other symptoms that the Game produces?

What are the Leverage Points in the Game?

What ideas, thoughts, emotions, beliefs, expectations, etc. operate as a leverage point in how the Game is set up?
If you wanted to change the Game, where's its weakest point?
What would be the easiest thing to do to mess up the Game?

What New Frame Game would you prefer to Play?

If you had a magic wand and could play a better, more empowering, more enhancing, and more productive Game, what Game would it be?

How would the New Frame Game go?

How would you play it?
With whom?
At what times?
How would you set up the new Game?

What would be the Objective of the New Frame Game?

What would be its outcome or goal?
Why would you play it?
What would be the outcome for the others?

How would we establish the New Game and Install it?

> If we can shift from the old to the new, how would that occur?
> If we have to reject the old entirely before initiating the new, how strong of a definitive "No!" do we need to say?
> What processes would help us to establish and solidify the new game?

Summary

- Life is all just a matter of *Games*—Games driven by frames.
- When you know how to view our actions and interactions in terms of Games, it puts you at choice with regard to what Games you'd like to play.
- We cannot *not* play Games. It's only a question of *what Games* we'll choose, and why.

Now That You Know—Here's What To Do

- Copy the Frame Game Analysis sheets and use them to analyze one or two of your most common Food Games.
- What new insights and resources do you discover as you use the Frame Game Analysis format?

Frame Games Worksheet — 1
Diagnosing a Toxic Game

1. *What's the Game?* Describe the "Game" being played out in terms of states meta-states, gestalt states. *What's the script of the Game?* What sub-Games or sub-frames are part of it all?

_____

_____

_____

2. *Cues & Clues:* What are some of the cues (linguistic, physical, environmental, etc.) that indicate the presence of a Game? How do you know? What cues you to it?

_____

_____

_____

3. *Players:* Who plays the Game? With whom? Who else has Games going on? What's the larger social system of the Game? (Use another Worksheet 1 for each additional person).

_____

4. *Hooks (triggers, baits):* What hooks you into the Game? How does the Game hook others to play?

_____

_____

_____

5. *Emotional Intensity of the Game:* How intense (0 to 10)? Are there any somatic responses or symptoms?

_____

6. *Rules of the Game:* How is the Game set up? How do you play? (Commands, Taboos)

_____

7. Quality Control: Do you like this Game? Just how sick is this Game? Ready to transform it?

_____

8. Agenda of the Game: What's the intention, motivation, or payoff of the Game? What's the payoff?

_____

9. Name the Frame Game:

_____

10. Style: What is your Frame of Mind? Style of thinking? Meta-Program or attitude?
> _ Matching / Mismatching   _ Reactive/ Thoughtful
> _ Fast/ Slow   _ Rigid / Flexible
> _ Aggressive/ Passive/Assertive   _ Self / Other
> _ Options/ Procedures   _ Global / Specific

11. Leverage points: Where is the leverage in this Game to stop it, change it, transform it?

_____

_____

_____

13. Preferred Frame Game: What Game would you rather play?

_____

Frame Games Worksheet — 2
Design Engineering a New Frame Game

1. **Desired** *Game:*

_____

2. *Target:* Name the person/s you want to influence (it will undoubtedly include yourself, it may even exclusively be yourself):

_____

3. *Emotional Agenda/Motivation:* What concerns, him or her most? Values? What's really important to this person? What would hook X into this Game? Vested interests?

_____

_____

_____

4. *Larger Systems:* What's the larger social system of the Game? Who else is involved?

5. *Objective and Outcome:* What do I want in this? What do I want for the other/s in this?

_____

_____

6. *Description:* How will the new Game be played? What frames will work best? Describe.

_____

_____

7. *Leverage points:* Where is the leverage to change or stop the Game? What frames will best leverage this person?

_____

_____

8. *Process:* How can I set up these frames? How can I implement my

persuasion process?

_____

_____

9. Check-list Stages: Will you need to interrupt, shift, loosen, and/or transform the frames? Which patterns or techniques would provide the most leverage?

_____

_____

10. Patterns for Installation: Which Frame Game (patterns) could you use to install the new Frame Games in yourself?

_____

_____

_____

_____

11. Frames: What frames of mind do you need in order to play the new Game?

_____

_____

PART II:

POWERING UP TO PLAY
FRAME GAMES

Chapter 4
The Power to Play

Chapter 5
Advanced Power for Playing

Chapter 6
Getting a Big Enough Why

Chapter 4

THE POWER

TO PLAY FRAME GAMES

"I'd like to play, but you see, I'm just too tired."

Have you ever attempted to play some Game, whether it be something vigorous like a gymnastic, swimming, or skiing or whether it be more cerebral like chess, monopoly, or cards and just didn't feel like you had the energy for it?

"I'm just too tired."

"I just don't feel up to it."

It takes energy to play. Maybe that's why kids play a lot more games than do adults. Fatigue in mind, emotions, and body can undermine our ability to play the more demanding and vigorous Games. When we get tired, depleted, or stressed, we become more vulnerable to another set of Games—the mental Games wherein we interpret the tiredness as meaning that we are unable, incapable, a victim, etc.

"I'm just not cut out for this! Pass me a donut!"

Concerning the Frame Games that govern how we play the Game of fitness, vitality, slimness, etc., it obviously takes mental and emotional energy, verbal and linguistic energy, behavioral and relating energy. We don't find *the excellence of slim fitness* in the lives of the lazy, the slothful, the indulgent, or the ones searching for "the path of least resistance." We find *the excellence of slim fitness* emerging in the lives of the passionate, the searchers for adventure, the dreamers who act, and those who love to rise up to meet a challenge.

'Hey, that sounded like a put-down to fat people!"

"Yeah, Do you think fat people are lazy and un-energetic, is that what you're saying?"

Take it easy guys. I mean no insult. Nor do I even want to go there. Why fuss and fume about any of that? Do you really want to play *that* Game? Suppose you "win" the argument or "lose" it? What will you gain from that? It's so easy to play Games of Distraction, of Blame, of Insult, etc.? Stay with me on this, I want to play a Game of Solution ... and it's going to take *energy*... it's going to involve the energy to say *"No!"* to yourself and your cravings, and it's going to involve the energy to say a much bigger *"Yes!"* to your goals and desired outcomes. If it helps you to think this means you have *not* been proactive and energetic, but lazy; then think such. If, on the other hand, it helps you to think that you've been energetic and that you have simply gotten over-weight or out-of-shape and that it had nothing to do with laziness; entertain those thoughts. Choose the interpretation that will best enable you to do something positive about it.

Frames for Energy

Frame Games thoroughly govern our lives. Every day we're playing *Frame Games* around food, eating, exercising, activities, etc. This means that we simply have to enter into the fray and actually *play* the Games if we want to achieve excellence in any field of endeavor. So, this raises some questions.

- Where do we find *the source of power* to play, to keep us alive and vigorous, and to keep rejuvenating our playfulness?

- What mechanisms govern the source of personal power to rise up to meet this challenge?

The **power** that enables us to frame, to create mind-body states, and to play the Games that we do are four in number. These involve *the two private powers* of thinking and feeling and it involves *the two public* *powers* of speaking and behaving. In and from these psychological and personal powers we can locate so many of the basic powers that support the mental, emotional, verbal, and behavioral powers that we need for thinking, choosing, creating mental models, representing and processing information, investing ourselves, valuing, generating meaning, and taking effective action.

In these mind-body powers (our neuro-linguistic powers) we have the source of all of the mental-and-emotional framing that we need to establish the Games that we want to play. After all, we *set frames* by the way we think, by what we think about, by the emotions that we evoke regarding those frames, and by how we then speak and act. These human functions enable us to play the *internal Head Games* and the *external Action Games.*

Figure 4:1

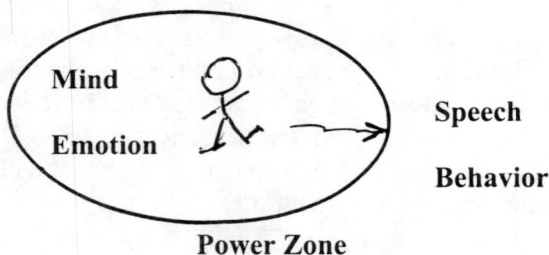

Mind

Emotion

Speech

Behavior

Power Zone

To "power up" to tap into and develop more energy for playing Frame Games with conscious mindfulness, we begin with this Game. We begin by recognizing and owning our core "powers" or functions, the functioning of our neurology and languaging (i.e., our neuro-linguistic functioning). By doing this, we will thereby establish the basis for *personal empowerment, responsibility, proactivity,* as well as many other higher level states that will make all the difference in the world in terms of our outcome of *business excellence.*

The "Powering Up" *Frame Game*

I like asking people about the *core* powers that supply and support all of our other powers.

"What are the most fundamental powers?"

"If you wanted to really *power up*, what would be the core powers that you'd focus your attention on?"

Many people don't know. They haven't been let in on the secret. When they hear the secret, they often discount it because they assume that it is too simple.

"What core powers can we access and then use at the higher levels of our mind for frame-setting?"

The answer partakes of a simplicity, yet a simplicity that's awesome in its profundity. It is this: we have four fundamental powers. Two occur deep inside and comprise our private powers and two occur more openly and comprise our public powers. Each of us have these *four* central and inescapable *powers*, which in turn, enable us with *the ability* to *respond* to things. Two of these human powers operate very privately (i.e., thinking and emoting) and two operate as our public contributions to the world (i.e., speaking and behaving). Herein lies our ability to cope and master the challenges that we face. Herein also lies the essence of our *response-ability*, that is, our ability or *power* to respond. These four powers as our core *Power Zone*.

1) *Thinking-feeling*.

In the private recesses of our mind we *think-and-feel*. Thinking-and-feeling makes up the central *engine* that drives all of the rest of our responses and gives shape to the very structure and affective tone of our "personality." And, just as certain as nobody can "make" you think a certain way without your consent, but can only invite you to try on a way of thinking, so nobody can "make" you feel a certain way. At best, others can invite, evoke, and provoke you to feel.

2) *Speaking and acting*.

We express our thoughts and feelings by *talking and acting*. These two public powers describe *how* we express ourselves. They put into our hands the power of effecting the outside world. We can do so by taking specific *actions* as an expression of our ability to give our thoughts and emotions a tangible and felt influence in the world. We can also talk, language, formulate ideas in linguistic forms from story, poetry, prose, new releases, books, problem solving, etc.   Herein lies our power to affect events, people, systems, etc. by using higher levels of symbols and affecting the minds and emotions of people.

"Power Zone" Ownership

If our most fundamental and core powers boils down to the processes of thinking-feeling, speaking and behaving, then there are only a couple questions left to ask.

- To what extent have you *recognized* these basic powers give you the ability to order and organize your own responses to the world? Your responses to food?
- To what extent have you fully *accepted and owned* these *powers* as your own?
- To what degree have you *cultivated and developed* these powers so that you experience them as vigorous?
- How much of these powers do you give away to others?

Figure 4:2

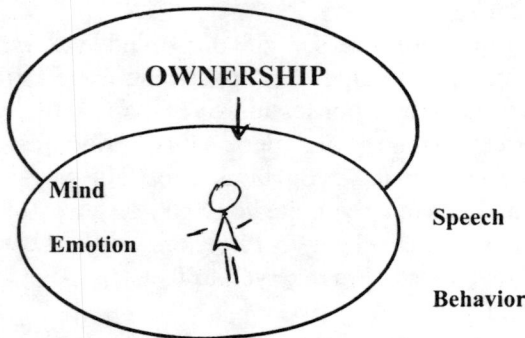

All of this points us to not only *accessing* our power zone, but *owning* it. It means embedding our sense of our personal powers inside of the frame of "Mine!" so that we cue our brain and nervous system to completely accept the powers. Doing so will empower us to then take initiate, become proactive, etc.

The Empowerment Frame Game

"Empowerment" has been a key word in both business and in personal development for the past couple decades. One term that expresses "empowerment" is *"proactivity."* Yet in all too many instances, these words have come *not* to stand for *actual and personal* powers of taking effective action, and doing so as an initiative rather than waiting for a crisis. More often than not, the words have been used as the latest business jargon to try to get employees more involved without actually empowering them.

True empowerment leads to a very different set of Games. It leads to managers and supervisors turning over the power and authority for making decisions in an area and then holding the persons responsible. It would lead to employees, managers, and others feeling the right, privilege, and responsibility to act, to significantly contribute, to move into a Solution Oriented frame of mind.

The same holds true for *true personal empowerment.*

When a person becomes truly and authentically **em-powered**, he or she now *has the ability to take effective action and make things happen.* The person with "power" can get him or herself to do what's desired, to avoid what's recognized as harmful, and to prepare for that action beforehand (pro-active).

• Would you like to play the *Empowerment Frame Game?*

• Would you like to develop your personal powers so that you can live your life and especially your life in relationship to eating and exercising in such a way that *you are in charge?*

To play this Game, we have to first of all recognize, accept, and own all of our *powers*, our powers of thinking-emoting, and of speaking and acting. This means adopting the following attitude.

"I, and only I, ultimately determine what I think and feel. Nobody can *make* me think or feel anything... I always play a determinative role about what I let into my mind and what I give attention to. I always have the power of mind and heart over this ultimate human freedom of what to think and how to think."

Do you *own* that way of playing the Game of Life? Would you like to? Would you like to say the same thing about your linguistic and behavioral powers?

> "I, and only I, ultimately determine what I say and how I say it, what I do, the actions I take, and the quality of the behaviors I use as I relate to the world of events and people. My actions and behaviors are mine just as my words, metaphors, stories, and language patterns, etc. By them I can make an impact on myself, on my world, and on others. I fully accept my power to influence others and do so responsibly."

Owning Our Power Zone Pattern

To fully and mindfully *own* our power zone, we need to do three things. First, *recognize* the existence of these powers. Next accept them, and then finally, *own* them. If you're ready to play, here's a pattern for making it real inside your mind-body system.

*1) Access and amplify the resource state of **Ownership.***

Think about a time or place when you strongly felt that something was yours. That it "belonged" to you. That you "owned" it free and clear. Think about something so that when that thing comes to mind, every fiber in your being, in your body, can fully and congruently say, **"Mine!"**

I would recommend that you keep your referent experience small and simple. Pick something like, "My hand!" "My eye." "My cat." "My pen." "My book." Stop now and try that on for size. If you have any difficulty with that, try "My toothbrush." "My underwear." If someone came up and said, "Could I use that toothbrush? Would you mind?" Do you immediately think, "Sure, go ahead." Or, does your mind go, "Well, I don't know, it's my toothbrush."

Now I have met some people who have theoretic concepts that will actually get in the way of accessing a simple sense of *ownership*. Perhaps they believe that "Nothing is mine, I'm just a pilgrim through this earthly pilgrimage." This shows how a higher frame sets the rules on the Games that we play. Invite them to recognize and accept that, "Yes, you are just a pilgrim or steward of these possessions, but they are *yours* to be treated with care. You are responsible for them, are you not?"

2) Apply that feeling of "Ownership" ("mine!") to your awareness of your Four Core Powers.

As you feel the sense of ownership, turn up those feelings so that they become stronger and stronger. Having picked some small and simple referent like "My toothbrush" enables us to obtain a pure and discreet sense of what ownership feels like. Make your pictures and sounds of that reference bigger, bolder, closer, etc. until you can feel that mind-body *state*. When you do, *apply that state* of thinking and feeling to your core powers.

Notice your power of thinking and say, "My thoughts, my brain, my mental processing!" Notice your power of feeling and emoting and say, "My emotions, my sensations in my body, my feelings, my investment of my heart, my bonding, attachment, caring, rejoicing, etc." Repeat this same process with speaking and behaving. "My words, my languaging, my use of symbols, my storytelling, my metaphors, etc." "My actions, my behaviors, my movements, gestures, and patterns of relating."

In so *owning* your core powers, gesture naturally and freely as if exploring about how to fully express the idea of *ownership* in the way you move your arms, breathe, stand, etc. Without the sense of ownership, we tend to treat things as interesting items to observe, talk about, and visit, but not fully use, take charge of, or embrace. Developmentally, we see the *ownership* stage in young children as they yell and asset themselves. They shout, "Mine!" and grab a toy, cookie, or crayon from another. But sometimes, unwitting parents will set out to beat this sense of *ownership* out of the child, confusing it with selfishness or something. They are not the same. So for some, re-claiming this power, granting oneself the right to *own* these powers, and asserting permission to do so will radically change the very structures of personality.

As you *feel the sense of ownership*, just revel and enjoy that as you apply to your core powers. Stay with that experience for a moment and then begin to notice the transformation of how you experience your thinking, emoting, speaking, and behaving when you fully *own* them as yours.

*3) Access states of **Acceptance and Appreciation** and apply to the state of Ownership.*

To enrich this one more time, let's do the following. Think about a small simple item that you "accept," and then another that you appreciate. In *acceptance*, you welcome into your world, but you don't particularly have to like it. You acknowledge it, you even embrace it, but you do so matter-of-factly and without much emotion. Think about accepting a rainy day, the traffic at rush hour, interruptions during the day, a baby messing his diaper—things like that. In *appreciation*, you not only welcome and embrace something, you do so with warmth, excitement, with a sense of seeing its value.   Think about the appreciation you have for a beautiful sunset, a warm bath, a card from a special one —things like that.

Again, access these experiences, feel the feelings that they initiate in your mind and body, and then just step into them even more fully, letting them grow stronger and more powerful. When they feel pretty intense (a 8 or 9 on a scale from 0 to 10), then *apply* that feeling to your sense of ownership. In this way you will set two higher frames *about* the ownership of your own power zone as you accept and then appreciate your core powers.

*4) Amplify all of these states until your **Neurology** begins to **Radiate.***

"I accept and appreciate these powers as mine... I welcome, receive, and warmly embrace these neuro-linguistic powers that give me the ability to take charge of my world. I appreciate and will continue to grow in appreciation for my thinking-and-feeling powers as an expression of how I can become much more effective in the world."

While you're at it, let your words emerge as you language this Powering Up Frame Game in as effective way as you can. Play with your words until you find those that really excite and give you a vision of the empowered you.

"This is my *zone* of power. I am totally responsible for my *responses* of mind, emotion, speech and behavior..."

5) Now imagine all of these thoughts and feelings and way of operating as you see yourself moving out into tomorrow and the days and weeks to come.

Vividly imagine taking the ownership of your essential powers with you to work, in the way you relate to others, in how you communicate, the energy and investment you put into your plan and goals, and every time you sit down to eat.

Validating the Game
   Did you like that?
   Would you like to even more fully recognize and own your own basic human powers so that you can take charge of your life?
   By asking questions that evoke a *"Yes"* response, I am not only seeking clarity, but also inviting you to *validate* the thinking, attitude, frames of mind, and their subsequent Games.   Asking rhetorical or straightforward *yes* questions has that effect.   In saying *"Yes,"* we essentially move up in our minds to *validate* an experience (a meta-cognitive move).
   Saying *"Yes"* to your mental and emotional powers will further build up a higher quality within you, one that we call *"ego-strength."*   This means the ability to use your ego sense (your sense of self, or I) to face reality for what it is and to look at it without blinking.   This also gives you the *ability* to affirm your values and visions and to dis-confirm things that do not fit or that violate what you consider important.   When you utter a *"Yes"* and/or a *"No"* to an experience, thought, choice, emotion, and response available to you, you have in your hands the dynamic-duo of *affirmation and disconfirmation*.   (We will explore that much more fully in the next chapter).   Recognizing that as you now say *"Yes"* to some things, you say *"No"* to other things allows you to control the inputs to your mind.
   What's the very first on the list of things to *Yes-and-No*?
   The *content* of your consciousness.
   What do you want to say *"Yes"* to in terms of the frames you want to

set? What do you want to say *"No"* to?

- What eating and exercising Games do you want to affirm? Which one would you like to disconfirm?
- What beliefs will you *"Yes,"* which will you *"No?"*
- What values and visions?
- What decisions and commitments?
- What self-definitions and identifications?
- What ideas and frames?

When you say *"Yes"* to your power zone, you say *"No"* to blaming, excuse-making, and irresponsibility. As a result, this will shift you from playing the *Blame Game* to the *Aim Game*. You will then focus on what you want to achieve—your aims and desired outcomes. When you don't get the responses you want, simply treat it as *feedback* (The Feedback Frame). You can then go into a learning mode (The Learning Frame) to discover what you can learn about how to do things differently. Then we shift your responses (The Flexibility Frame Game) and keep varying your speaking and acting responses until you get the response that you want (The Persistence Frame Game).

Owning Our Personal Power
Means Assuming Responsibility

Something "more than the sum of the parts" of the human mind-body system arises when we *own* our personal power zone. We call this larger emerging gestalt, *Responsibility.* This higher level frame of mind serves as the foundation for the actual "cure" of being over-weight. Frank Laverty (1977), using T.A. (Transactional Analysis), the "Games People Play" model said this:

"A cure is possible only if you accept that you are totally responsible for your feelings and actions. Others cannot make you feel good or bad nor can they make you behavior in any particular way. You and you alone make the decision. ... We are influenced by others, but the final decision is ours.

Many obese people avoid accepting responsibility for their condition by transferring or projecting the responsibility to other people." (p. 19)

Here are the Games that Laverty said they play:

I'm overweight because Jean cooks rich food.
I eat dessert to please Sally.
I wouldn't eat chocolates if Jack didn't buy them for me.
I eat seconds because Paul hates to waste food.
I have a couple of drinks before dinner because Tom doesn't enjoy drinking alone.

Then he comments,

"People who take full responsibility for their feelings and behavior are able to say 'no' to excess food without feeling guilty or sorry. This does not mean that a person will not have bad feelings; it means only that he makes the final decision about what, when, and how long to feel bad... Refusing to accept responsibility is a learned part of an overweight person's program. ... You alone are responsible for your excess weight." (p. 20)

Empowered to Reject the Blame Game

Intellectually, it's fairly easy to recognize, realize, and accept that *nobody can "make" you angry.* Your anger is your own. It arises from your angry thoughts and angry state. Your loneliness is also yours, as is your sadness, stress, discouragement, and every other negative emotion that you might use as a trigger to sooth and comfort yourself by eating.

It becomes much more difficult to practice this higher level of consciousness in the presence of someone who seems to know how to "push all of your buttons" and get under your skin. How can we say *"No"* to the Blame Frame Game when it feels so pleasurable to blame?

Here clarity provides us a great deal of our strength. Being crystal clear about owning our power zone and having mentally, verbally, and behaviorally practiced a set of effective responses enables us to say *No* to defaulting to the Blame Frame.

Certainly, others can *invite* us to feel angry and upset. To do that, they have to communicate or act in such a way so as to provoke us into *thinking* upsetting thoughts. If we buy into their frame, it becomes inevitable that we will *feel upset.* Others can provide incredibly powerful stimuli that invites, urges, provokes, incites, and elicits upsetting thinking-and-emoting responses from us. Yet our *response* is always that —our response. It begins with a mental response and it shows up as a behavioral response.

We can only play the *Blame Frame Game* by failing to distinguish between *the stimulus* that others offer and *our response*. There is a difference. One describes the trigger; the other describes the response. When I *think* that I have no choice, that I *have to* get angry, I thereby give my power away. I have become the other person's slave, doing his or her bidding. Doing so dis-empowers me, and then I become a victim.

Listen to the frames that people set that sends them into the Blame Frame Game:

> "My husband (wife) makes me so angry (upset, worried, etc.) that I just can't stand it! He drives me to eating."

> "I know that she uses that tone of voice with me when we talk about finances (children, in-laws, work, etc.), it makes me feel put-down and degraded. I just hate the way she controls me. No wonder I never eat right"

> "I had to retaliate in the way I did, he made me feel worthless. How can I think about my health or fitness when things like that go on?"

This kind of talk assumes that the speaker has no power, no choice, and no response-ability. When we talk that way, no wonder we become *reactive.* We have no other choice. Our frame induces us to live in a deterministic world. As long as we *frame our thinking to believe* that others control our responses, that frame will govern our states.

To play the *Empowerment Frame Game* we shift to a new way of thinking-and-feeling. We proactively recognize and own our *powers*.

> "My responses of thought and emotion result from the way *I think and emote.* No one 'makes' me think in a certain way. My thoughts arise from how I choose to think. No one 'makes' me feel in certain ways. My emotions also arise from my thinking and valuing. I will not play the victim and give all my power away to them."

Summary

- It takes *energy* to play Games; it takes power to play *Frame Games,* mental energy, emotional energy, verbal energy, physical energy, personal energy. When we're depleted, others can more easily play Games with us without our awareness or ability to stand up to the Games and refuse them.

- The core of personal power resides in our neuro-linguistic powers of thinking, feeling, speaking, and behaving. These are essential and fundamental. They arise from our innate neurological and linguistic processes.

- We begin to play the first Game that will build and support our business excellence when we recognize, accept, own, and validate our Power Zone.

Now That You Know—Here's What To Do

- Play the Ownership Game to power-up with your most fundamental powers. Find someone in your life who will be game to play this Game with you. By coaching someone else through the Ownership of My Powers Game, you'll find it more integrated into your own life.

- Are there any Games that you have to reject and refuse in order to claim ownership of your powers? Identify those frames and/or games.

Chapter 5

ADVANCED POWER

FOR PLAYING

Developing High Quality Octane Power

Games in this Chapter
The Affirmative "Yes!"
The Refusal Game of "No!"

"Do you feel up to playing a Game of chess with me?"
"Yeah, that's fine."
"Are you sure?"
"Yeah, I can get through it."

Now that ought to be an exciting Game!
Not.

It not only takes energy to play Games. In fact, it takes *vigorous* energy, *vibrant* energy, *definitive* energy. It takes the kind of energy that allows us not to "just get through it," but to have a ball in the process. And that's the kind of power we need to become fit and slim, isn't it?

The power to play begins by accessing, owning, and validating our basic core powers, those neuro-linguistic powers that enable us to take charge of our lives, run our own brains, and determine our own pathway toward excellence. As you have now discovered and practiced *accessing your power zone*, that zone of energy in which you can *center* yourself in knowing and experiencing your ultimate freedom, the freedom to determine *what* you think and *how* you think... which then, in turn, puts increased mastery into your hands over your emotions, languaging, and acting.

While that's a great beginning, it doesn't end there. In fact, by refreshing our awareness, appreciation, and use of these thinking-and-emoting powers, linguistic and behavioral powers, we have just begun in putting them to use, not only at the primarily level of everyday experience, but at all of the higher levels of mind.

Playing the Game of Validation

I invited you to play the *Validation Frame Game* in the previous chapter when I simply asked you questions that presupposed a *"Yes!"* answer. Now what were those questions? Oh, yes:

*   Did you like that?
*   Would you like to even more fully recognize and own your own basic human powers so that you can take charge of your life?

What happens when we ask any question that invites a natural and strong *Yes* response? Notice for yourself:

*   Would you like to increase your personal skills and competency?
*   Would you like to become more intelligent in the way you think, make decisions, and respond?
*   Would you really like to increase your wealth and influence with people?
*   Really?
*   Would you find that valuable?

"Yes" eliciting questions obviously put us into a particular *frame of mind* that accesses a unique mental-and-emotional state. What frame of mind does it induce in you? Where do you go? What do you feel?

"Yes" questions, especially strong ones that activate our highest values, goals, beliefs, and purposes, typically elicits in us a sense of *affirming, validating, and confirming.* In saying and feeling *"Yes!"* we access a state of mind wherein we feel affirmative. Saying *"Yes"* puts our mind and body into a place where we are much more ready to do something about our *"Yes."* It activates our motor programs from which

we take action.

Sales people have known this for a long time. They call it *"the Yes set."* They work to get a person to say *"Yes"* seven times in a row because they know that once in that state, that mode, that orientation, it will be more difficult for them to shift suddenly to a "No." *"Yes"* elicits a state of confirming that creates this motor response, this neuro-linguistic orientation.

Notice also the positive sense of direction that simple word *Yes* can provoke. In saying *"Yes"* to something, we develop more of a positive orientation, a solution orientation, a proactive sense of taking action to fulfill our dreams and outcomes. And it makes sense, doesn't it? To say *"Yes"* is to *validate*, and in *validating* we come close to making a pledge, a promise, a commitment.

> "Yes, I will ... give myself to becoming much more resourceful and productive."

Doesn't that feel good? Isn't there a basic healthfulness and robustness to saying *"Yes"* to a valued objective or a valued belief? It seems that when we rise up in our minds to affirm with a hearty *"Yes,"* we rise up to access some of our highest levels of mind. We become more ... it brings out the best in us.

> "Wouldn't you like to experience that kind of state on a daily basis?"

> "Wouldn't that create an ongoing and rejuvenating sense of purpose and meaning, and wouldn't that revitalize your energy?"

Ah, and that's what this Frame Game is all about. As we learn how to truly affirm, we learn how to amplify our basic powers. The fabulous thing, of course, is that we have to use our thinking, representing, valuing, emoting, speaking, and acting powers to access this power.

The Magic of Saying *"Yes!"*

Saying *"Yes,"* (especially a strong and vigorous *"Yes"!)* enables us to establish higher frames of mind about things as well as to solidify those frames. You might have noticed this with the exercise in the previous chapter. Once you have recognized, accepted, and appreciated your "power zone," and accessed a strong, or maybe the strongest representation you have of a strong and over-whelming **"Yes!"**, you can then connect that sense of confirmation to your power zone. Imagine that. You can then embrace the first *"Yes!"* inside an even higher series of "Yeses!" as frames of confirmation.

> "Yes, by God, it's my zone wherein I do have the power to respond, to think, to imagine, to create, to feel, to connect, to invest myself, to love, to celebrate, to talk, to put ideas into language, to act on my beliefs..."

And that sense of validating your core powers then generates a sense of what we call *self-efficacy*, the confidence in your own competence to be efficient, effective, and able to take effective action. Would you like that as your everyday frame of mind— a frame of mind to wake up in and operate from? Really?

Getting Your Vigorous "Yes!"

The idea of saying *"Yes"* to something gives voice to confirming, validating, and affirming. It's one of our most basic states, a primordial power, one of our primary states, a developmental stage that we all negotiated when we were very young, and one in which some people have suffered damage. That is, their *ability to affirm* has been lost or weakened. Numerous experiences can make it difficult to think and feel in an affirmative way, and can tempt us to create various mental maps that prevent us from experiencing affirmation: disappointments, frustrations, confusions, failure to be loved and valued, traumas, etc.

Let's refresh our ability to affirm. Here's an exercise to renew and rejuvenating this *Yes-ing* power.

1) Access a discreet and intense referent that you can purely "Yes!"

What can you say *"Yes!"* to with every fiber of your being? What brings out the biggest, strongest, wildest, and most powerful *"Yes!"* in you? Would winning a millionaire dollars? Would recovering your youthful energy? Would touching a loved one's life with some real healing power?

Think of something you can absolutely say *"Yes!"* to in the most powerful way possible. Once you've done that, access four more references for an empowering *"Yes."*

Find your referent and then let yourself feel that *"Yes"* fully and completely. Stay with it and experience it in all of the sensory systems: visually (the sights and images), auditorially (the sounds, tones, volumes, music, words), and kinesthetically (the physical sensations in your body, warmth, excitement, relaxation, etc.). As you stay with the feelings and let them grow, allow yourself to gesture with your arms and hands, even with your full body. How do you gesture a strong and vigorous *"Yes?"* What does *"Yes!"* look like, sound like, feel like in your movements, etc.? You may even want to experiment with finding seven different tonalities for uttering your *"Yes!"* Utter a series of three yeses, each with a rising crescendo of intensity and emphasis, **"Yes, Yes!, YES!"** Continue to juice up your *"Yes"* until you begin to drool!

2) Apply your sense of "Yes" to your Core Powers.

When you have the biggest and most ferocious *"Yes!"* that you can experience today (knowing, of course, that it will double and triple in intensity in the days to come), bring this *"Yes! "* to bear upon (that is, *apply it to)* your *awareness* of your sense of personal power and mastery. Say *"Yes!"* to the idea of taking charge of your life and becoming proactive in the way you live it. Validate that as a concept, as a belief, as a value. Confirm it repeatedly in as many ways as you desire to confirm it.

When you have confirmed it thoroughly, read and answer with a *"Yes!"* the following questions, or better, have a friend read them to you.

- Do you really want that idea in your head?
- Would you want it in your body?
- Would you like it in every muscle of your body?
- Would you like it as your way of being in the world?
- Would it enhance your life?
- Would it make you a better person?
- Would it contribute to your everyday experiences?
- Would it enrich your work and career?
- Would it begin to develop your genius at work?

3) Confirm the Confirmation.
So you really would want this? You're not kidding me about this? You are fully okay with becoming more empowered? You really want to say yes to that?

Yes-ing our ideas, concepts, understandings, and beliefs enables us to set an even higher frame of validation on our validation. And in doing that, we solidify our frames. This embeds our thoughts within a frame of confirmation and elicits within us reasons for the validation. So just keep right on *"Yes-ing"* these ideas and representations until you begin to hear a matter of fact voice commenting on your inner movie and saying, "Why, yes, of course!"

"Yes-ing" Yourself into New Beliefs

We call this the Meta-*Yes*-ing Pattern and use it as a belief change process. A "belief" change pattern? Yes.

"I don't understand. What's the connection between saying, *"Yes"* and "believing?"

Can you *think* of something without *believing* it?

Can you read something in the local newspaper, hear something on television, talk with a friend about his or her different point of view, understand with clarity and precision that different opinion and still *not* believe it?

Can you listen with appreciation to a discussion of business ideas and alternatives and come away still not *believing* that's the way the company ought to go?

Yes, I know, rhetorical questions. Of course, you can *think* without believing. You'd be in a poor place (mentally and emotionally) if you *believed* everything you saw, heard, or read! If course, some people *seem* to live their lives that way. They won't read, view, or think in any depth about anything that they don't agree with and believe in.

If we can fully and completely represent, encode, and understanding data without believing it, then what's the difference? What's the difference between a "thought" and a "belief?"

In Neuro-Semantics, we have discovered that a "thought" remains just a thought if we do *not* confirm it. Conversely, as we *confirm* a thought, we turn or transform that thought into a "belief." A belief then exists as something more than a mere thought, it involves two levels of awareness. On the first level, there is a thought, then above and beyond that there is the level of confirmation. When these levels come together and merge, we have a *confirmed and validated thought.* This means that a mental-emotional transformation occurs when we confirm and validate an idea. What once was just a representation now becomes "something more than the sum of the parts." It becomes an energized, dynamic "belief," a command to the nervous system to actualize and make real the content of the belief.

This *structure* of a belief explains why beliefs operate as self-fulfilling prophecies in our minds and bodies. It explains the power of beliefs as well as the danger of beliefs. It explains why we experience a mere "thought" as innocent and harmless, but when we turn it into a belief, it can change a person inside-out. Beliefs become higher frames of mind and operate as the governing influence in a living system that will self-organize after the image and likeness of the belief. (You can find a lot more written about this in *The Structure of Excellence* 1999, Hall and Bodenhamer.)

Blowing Out Old Beliefs by Meta-*No-ing*

The converse of saying *"Yes"* to something is to say *"No."* And as *"Yes"* confirms and validates, *"No"* dis-confirms and dis-validates. As *"Yes"* turns thoughts into beliefs, so *"No"* undoes the gestalt and reduces a belief to a harmless mere thought. *"No"* invites us to play an entirely new Frame Game. By finding, accessing, and applying a definitive *"No!"* we can refuse *Frame Games* and use our core powers to set boundaries and limits on the Games that others can play with us.

Now there's a funny thing about beliefs. You can learn better. You can gain new knowledge and awareness that updates your old maps from some old outdated or toxic belief, and yet, *you can still act and feel as if you believe it.* It's a strange phenomenon. You "know" intellectually that criticism will not hurt you, but when you experience it, you act and feel *as if* it's the worst thing in the world, *as if* you've been slugged in the stomach.

What gives?

Probably an old belief. Probably an old belief operating outside-of-conscious awareness.

So how can we use a nicely placed *"No"* to blast out such old and/or toxic beliefs that still run the show? How can we disconfirm that old frame and completely reject it, fire it, decommission it?

Once we have detected such a belief frame, especially a pathetic belief that only sickens the mind or spirit and creates a crappy attitude, how can we say a definite and resounding *"No!"* to it so that it blows to smithereens?

In a word we access a state of *"No!"* a state or frame of mind wherein we can reject and dis-confirm. It's a strong mind-body state. For it you will need to find a very strong and definitive **"No!"**

1) *Access and amplify a strong Dis-confirmation state.*

Think of something to which every fiber of your being can say *"Hell No!"* and do so fully and completely. Identify five different items to which you feel a strong, powerful, and definitive **"No!"**

As you do, access each experience separately and as discreetly as possible. Again, as with the *"Yes,"* gesture with your hands, arms, and full body in such a way that you shove away from you, and your "space," that old toxic belief.

Upon accessing this *"No!"* each time, *amplify* it so that it feels stronger and stronger in your neurology, and continue to do this until every fiber of your being wants to shout out with all of the energy that you can muster, *"Hell, No!"*

2) *Enjoy and relish this power to Stubbornly Refuse things.*

When you get all of that definitive energy pumped up so that it energizes you thoroughly in mind-and-body, take a moment to *enjoy* this power of refusal, disconfirmation, rejection, and stubbornness. *Relish* in this power of self-determination to have the final word about what you will and what you will not admit entrance into your mental and emotional space.

Your parents or teachers or others in early life may have tried to beat this power out of you, so be it. That was then. Today is now. And today you can give yourself permission to have the right, the privilege, and the responsibility to say "No." It's never too late to access and develop the personal resources we need for effectively navigating life. Refuse to whine, and learn to say *"No"* in a powerful way!

3) Apply this dis-confirmation to the toxic belief.

Holding all of these feelings of *"No!"* constant, begin to direct them to every belief, idea, activity, etc. that you want to utter a final and definitive "No!" to. Bring this neurological *"No!"* to bear upon various toxic ideas, beliefs, behaviors, and habits. As this *"No!"* becomes a *meta-no* to the experience that you will no longer tolerate, repeat the *"No!"* until you feel it pushing away the unenhancing state ... do so until this neurological *"No!"* becomes a matter-of-fact "No." "No, of course, not. Are you crazy? Why would I want *that*?"

There are some really sick Games. There are some really sick ideas, thoughts, beliefs, and frames. Is there any idea, experience or Game that you'd like to refuse right now? Feel that "No!" about that.

The Power to Say "No!"

Now with this power, you can use your mental-emotional energies to refuse things, to set boundaries, to establish limits, to differentiate yourself from others, to individualize, to discover and create your own identity, etc.

Developmentally, we all experience two periods of life where we have to engage in saying *"No"* in order to individualize and differentiate as we learn to become our best selves. We do this during "the terrible twos" and during the turbulent storms of adolescence. These developmental stages enable us to differentiate in order to create the kind and quality of *independence* so that we can become healthily *inter*-dependent later.

But, of course, lots of parents didn't graduate from *Parenting #101* and so failed to understand the importance and value of such differentiation. They took the *"No-ing!"* of their children as personal and so squelched it in their kids or tried beat it out of them. They forbid their kids the right to say *"No."* And lots of kids grew up with a taboo rule about saying *"No."* This led them to begin to play *the Frame Game* of non-assertiveness as they learned to fear of their own strength. The taboo frame forbid them from knowing their own mind, emotions, values, strengths, etc. Permission to do this was taken away from them. Years later, of course, they find themselves feeling like wimps, beaten pups, like jello personalities with no fiber of will, no will power, no determination or persistence to go after their own visions and values. It's not a very fun Game to play.

Summary

- If we really want to develop mastery in playing the Games of life and the Games necessary for the Slim Games, we have to have the twin abilities to say *"No!"* to sick and toxic things, and to less valued choices, and the ability to say a full and affirmative *"Yes!"* to the things that fulfill our vision of all the good things in being fit and slim.

- Affirming and dis-affirming, validating and dis-validating puts into our hands the very powers that can transform inspiring thoughts into full-fledged *beliefs* and that can unglue the danger of old beliefs that no longer serve us.

- Recognizing that *beliefs* represent a higher level of mind than mere *thought* alerts us to the fact that thoughts differ. There are *levels of thoughts.* And the higher thoughts become beliefs and frames of mind and they are the mechanisms that really govern the Games that we play. And therein lies even higher power!

Now That You Know—Here's What To Do

- Practice the *"Hell, No!"* Game repeatedly throughout this week. Notice this week also how you do have the power to say "No" to some things and to refuse some things from having any place or space in your life. Catch this power so you can amplify it and use it powerfully in your life.

- Practice the *"Heaven, Yes!"*Game as well. Reclaim your power to affirm, to validate, and to welcome exciting new things into your life. Rent the movie,

Harry Meets Sally, and especially the restaurant scene to get a great sense of saying "Yes, Yes, Yes!"

THE POWERS OF "YES!" AND "NO!"

ON THE SURFACE,
THEY SEEM SO SIMPLE, OBVIOUS,
AND COMMONPLACE.
HOW COULD
OUR BASIC HUMAN POWERS
ARISE FROM "YES!" AND "NO!"?

YET
WITHIN THESE SIMPLE WORDS
LIE OUR POWERS
FOR
AFFIRMING & DISCONFORMING,
VALIDATING & DISVALIDATING,
FOR CLEARING SPACE
& WELCOMING NEW REALITIES
INTO OUR MINDS, HEARTS,
AND SOULS.

Chapter 6

DEVELOPING
YOUR
GREAT BIG *WHY*

You Have To Have a Big Enough WHY
To Transform Your Habits of
Eating & Exercising

Games in This Chapter:
Getting a Great Big Why Game
The Intentional Stance Game

In every program of change and transformation from one Game in life to another Game, there has to be sufficient motivation. Do you have sufficient motivation for playing the Slim Game?

- Are you sufficiently motivated to quit the old food Games and adopt some new games?
- Do you feel highly motivated to say *"No!"* to the old Games that you know don't work and *"Yes!"* to some new Games?
- How much intensity of motivation, passion, and desire do you have?
- Why do you want to get your act together about eating and exercising?
- Do you have a *big enough why* to carry the day?

"Will power" is greatly misunderstood. Lots of people, perhaps most people, who feel stuck, unable to make effective changes, and who doubt that anything will *really* work, have mapped that they are somehow lacking in "will power."   This is as ignorant as it is pernicious. It is ignorant because it misunderstands what "will power" is and how it works.

The *power* of *will* involves two key psychological factors: Attention and Intention. Typically we experience the "work" of will power in the effort it takes to make our *attentions* to stay with our *intentions*. We set positive and wonderful intentions about eating right, exercising regularly, controlling what we eat, the amount we eat, etc., and then when it comes time to actually do the right thing, we seem to be of another mind. It seems hard in the midst of real world constraints, temptations, and situations to keep our attention on the things that we thought we wanted.

What's the problem?

How come we find our "good intentions" slipping and sliding?

What grabs and captures our attentions?

Attention and Intention

Whether you know it or feel it, we experience these two facets of "mind" on different levels. *Attention* is what's immediately in front of us and "on" our mind. To elicit our attentions, we only have to ask:

What are you attending?

What are you aware of?

What is grabbing your attentions?

Attentions describes mind in the present moment. It describes the what is on the "screen of our consciousness" in the current situation. It describes the movie playing in our mind. That's why we experience our attentions in terms of the triggers and stimuli in the immediate environment.

"I couldn't help it. When I saw all that food on the table, I just lost control."

"Did you see *that* cake*?!*"

"I couldn't concentrate with *that* music in the background."

"The smells of the place were overwhelming."

"I wanted to pay attention to what I was eating, but the worries about my finances kept intruding."

At the primary level of experience, *attentions* describe and define the functioning of mind-and-emotion as it encounters the environment. *Attentions* make up the things "on our mind." It's part of the stimulus-response world that we live in.

Yet our mind involves more than just attentions. It involves intentions. *Intentions* occur at a higher level. *Intentions* describes the things "in the back of the mind" and the things "in the uppermost of our mind." At this level we experience our chosen values, understandings, goals, outcomes, etc. Here we set a direction or orientation for ourselves—where we want to go.

But then we return to the primary state of immediate awareness and the higher awarenesses seem to vanish, to be overwhelmed by immediate sensory stimuli. Despondently, we invent verses to encode our cynicism about will power, "The path to hell is paved with good intentions."

Actually this description gives us an entirely false impression about what's really going on. It's false because it takes a snapshot of a moment in time and so takes the relationship between attention and intention *out of context.*

What is the larger context?

What is the true relationship between intention and attention?

Backing Up for a Larger View

From the snapshot viewpoint, it seems that *attention* is much more powerful and dominating than intention. Don't believe it. It is not. There is much more power in intention. The problem isn't that attention can and does override intention, it's that we have already set *other intentions* and that our *new intentions* are not sufficiently established or set. The true problem is that the older intentions have already been set —and that the everyday *attentions* are doing what attentions do best, they act as the perceptual radar for the higher intentions.

Typically, we "chose" a great many (perhaps most) of our highest intentions by default. We made our "chosen" by just absorbing the typical cultural values as we were culturalized and socialized. The result is that we don't experience our "mind" as belonging so much to ourselves. Instead, we experience our mind as just running its preprogrammed programs. The so-called "attention deficit" that we experience is really a problem of "intention deficit." We have simply *not* taken charge of setting higher intentions in a way that have made them stick. We continue to default to the cultural programs that we have absorbed.

> "The path of least resistance makes life easier."
> "I want it all!"
> "I cannot *not respond* to things in my environment."
> "It's impolite to screen things out and to become highly focused."
> "But what if I miss something really good?"

Typically, these are the *intentions* that are really running the show. These frames of mind govern the everyday attentions that we experience. And they may prevent other *intentions* from getting set.

In mind, higher intentions always govern. That's how true "will power" works. Once we set something in our mind, it establishes a self-organizing influence so that the way we perceive, talk, act, feel, etc. does service to that intentional frame. It operates as the Boss of all of our immediate attentional thoughts. It gives instruction regard what we attend.

Will power occurs and operates over a much long period of time. So as we step back to look at all of the hundreds and thousands of small choices about what to read, think, talk about, respond to, etc., these are the small everyday steps by which we have *set our intentions.* By them, we establish a direction— an orientation. By them, we establish a set of priorities, understandings, values, criteria, standards, beliefs, etc.

While this typically occurs without a lot of awareness, we can do it mindfully. In fact, to consciously choose our highest intentions enables us to live much more purposefully. It enables us to take an intentional stance in life and to align all of our attentions with our highest intentions. And when we do that, we then experience the subjective sense of having a lot of "will power." We feel in control of our minds, emotions, and responses. We feel "at choice." It's a great feeling.

Eliciting Your Highest Intentions

As we separate *attention and intention*, we recognize the *two-layered nature* of mind or will. This then opens our eyes to realize that *behind* and *within* every thought, there are things that we *attend to* in the front of our mind and things which we *intend* at the back of our mind or in the uppermost part of our mind. The things "on our mind" highlight our focus—our focus of attention. Then, above and beyond that attention, at a higher level, we have *intentions*—the highest things that we truly seek to achieve. At this level, we have our motives, agendas, reasons, etc.

Personal mastery emerges as we mindfully align our *attentions* so that they fit with our higher *intentions*. This allows us to take an intentional stance in the way we move through life, going after what we deem as important and valuable. Then, when we choose a way of thinking, feeling, acting, eating, exercising, etc., we can make it happen. It's not "will power" in the old Victorian sense of forcing ourselves against ourselves, it is a much kinder and gentler approach, an approach that respects these different facets and dimensions of our consciousness.

In attention, we *represent* whatever is on the immediate screen of our mind. We see this or that food, the clock, and other things that cue us about eating. At this level of mind, our *attentions* seem very volatile, shifting, impermanent, and elusive. Our attentions come and go. Our stream of consciousness rises and falls with the currents of the immediate environment. Things, people, and events "catch our attention." So we look. Here *mind* seems weak, fragile, ever-shifting, deficient in powerful focusing. At this level, the shiftings of mind operate as if we are moving through the world channel surfing. And, perhaps that's precisely what we're doing—jumping from one channel of awareness to another.

This describes how we all, typically, experience our primary level *attentions*. This is good. There's nothing wrong or pathological about the ever-shifting nature of our stream of consciousness. This does *not* mean that we have *Attention Deficit Disorder.*

Figure 6:1

Higher
Meta-Levels　　　　　　Intention of Intention
　　　　　　　　　　　Higher level Purposes, Agendas

Meta-Level　　　　　　Intention: Aim, Purpose, Outcome

Primary Level　　　　　Everyday States — **attending to**
　　　　　　　　　　　　　　　　this or that —|> 　Object/ Event
　　　　　　　　　　　　　　　　　　　　　　　　In the World

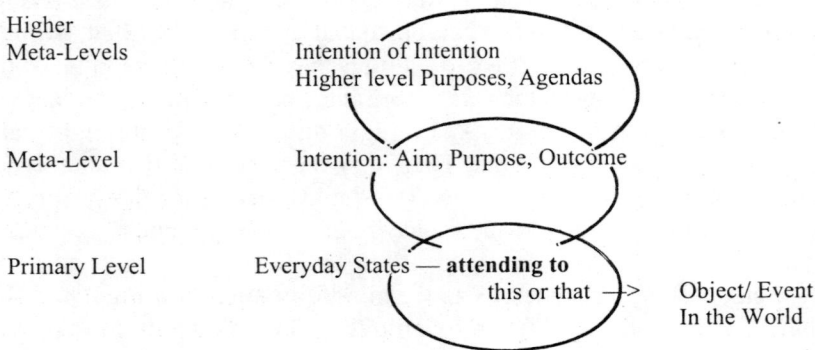

At higher or meta-levels, we experience our *intentions*. And because our *intentions* operate at a higher level, they are more stable and lasting. Except in times of indecision, we don't find our *intentions* shifting all over the place. When that occurs, we experience a painful sense of internal conflict over basic values, beliefs, understandings, etc.

"Do I want this or that? Why can't I have both? I kind of want this. But then again, I also want this other."

Actually, we seldom experience our *intentionally driven attentions* as separate functions. We experience them together as a complete gestalt, as our functioning mind. The thoughts in the back of our mind combine with the thoughts in the front of our mind. To us, it usually seems as one thing—consciousness.

Whenever an attended concept, or set of representations, does not seem to work in terms of making us more resourceful in moving on in life, we can now shift our focus. We can identify our higher and highest intentions and then align our everyday attentions with them. Or, we can establish new and higher positive intentions which will then govern new attentions. This will de-energize old attentions, slay demons, tame dragons, and create a powerful new focus of excellence in life.

Attempting to *only* deal with *attention*, without working with our *intentions* at the same time blinds us from ever finding the leverage points by which we can transform things. It also mis-focuses our energies. We end up fighting with our attentions— trying to get them to go away. And that's a battle we will not win.

We all have the ability to become distracted and to engage in mental *channel surfing* with their minds. Add a little stress, some negative experience, some conflicting values, etc., then try to concentrate!

Most of us actually suffer from *intention deficit*. We lack a strong *intention*, or reason, for staying with our goals and objectives. We have not developed *a strong enough why*. Unlike the person who strongly *wants* some particular knowledge or information, and knows precisely what they will do with it, how it will enrich their life, what it will make them, etc., our *intention deficit* causes us to waver.

Unless we take charge of our *intentions* by setting up higher level frames of references, our attentions will simply go into "channel surfing" mode. They will race here and there. They will be grabbed by this movement, that color, and this compelling representation. Like a wild and undisciplined monkey, it will be all over the place playfully checking things out and staying with none for long.

Consider the powerful persuaders who design commercials. What incredible artists at "capturing attention" by vivid, dramatic, and surprising sights and sounds. They turn on loud dramatic sounds that demand that we look up to see what's happening. "Made you look!" they say. They use the most momentary pictures of provocative and curious sights that leave us on the edge of our seats or a cliff just waiting for more. They change the view every couple of seconds. And, a steady diet of that kind of way of thinking can invite us to install inside of our own representational screen an ever-shifting "commercial consciousness."

Live your life with that kind of mind and you'll feel helpless and unable to direct your own mind. Live like that and then try to control your eating. Good luck!

Conversely, when we *align our attentions **to our higher intentions**,* then we use (and commission) our motivations, reasons, values, beliefs, higher level interests, etc. to govern and control our *attentions*. Doing this empowers us with a sense of personal mission and purpose. The higher frames then operate as attractors in a self-organizing system. The higher *intention* (and intention of that intention, etc.) become our highest level "program."

When Cindy Took an Intention Stance

I used this approach when I first met Cindy. She was in her late 20s, a mother of two boys, and sixty pounds overweight. She came to me after trying Weight Watchers and several dieting programs. After taking some personal history, especially the history of what Cindy had tried that did *not* work, I began by asking, "If you will indulge me, I want to ask you a series of questions that you will probably think are obvious and don't need to be asked. But if you will indulge me, I do want to ask some questions about your intentions."

"Okay."

"Good. Tell me what you want... What you really want to achieve by our visits together."

"Well, I want to lose weight. ... I want to lose sixty pounds and get back to what I weighed before the children came."

"That sounds like a legitimate goal and a highly valued one."

"Oh, it is."

"Well tell me Cindy, what will it do for you when you lose that weight? What will you get when you get that?"

"What will I get? ... I will get... ah, my proper weight. ... and I'll look better."

"Great. Losing extra pounds will enable you to look better. And when you get that, how is that important to you?"

"Well, I want to look better."

"Certainly, and why?"

"Because that will raise my self-esteem."

"That sounds important to you. How is that important? What will you get when you look better, have a greater sense of self-esteem?"

"Well, I will be able to get back to doing some of the things I use to do, ski, even rollerblade."

"Is that what higher self-esteem will do for you or is that another reason for losing the weight?"

"For losing the weight. Definitely. And I'll also be able to wear lots of the clothes I really look good in."

"So you have three reasons for losing weight: look better, fit into the clothes that you like, and get back to some of the activities you used to do. Anything else?"

"That's about it."

"And when you get all of that, getting that enables you to feel better about yourself, to experience higher self-esteem?"

"Yes."

"Great. Then imagine having all of that. Imagine having all of that fully and completely and in just the way you want it... Be there with those feelings. Got it? [Yes.] Good. Now when you get all of that in that way, what does that do for you? How is that important? What do you get from that?"

".... [pause] ... I get a sense of being in charge of my own life. Like I'm able to do what I want to."

"Great. And that seems important. [Yes, it is.] And how is that important? What do you get then?"

"When I feel in charge of my own life, ah ... I feel empowered, assertive, ah ... just more in control of my destiny ..."

"And how is that valuable to you?"

"I feel more true to myself, like I have personal integrity."

"And how is that important to you?"

"Then I feel right, right with God, right with the world..."

"Great. Do you feel that? Imagine allowing yourself to have all of this full and completely so that you can feel that to the degree that you want to... and just be with that feeling.... Got it? [Yes.] ... Good. Now take that feeling and breathe it into every fiber of your being, into your eyes, into your posture, into your muscles, your muscle tension, into how you move ... And imagine taking this feeling with you into your everyday activities of eating, drinking, preparing meals, exercising, etc. And as you do, just notice how this transforms things..."

"Do you like that?"

"Oh yes!"

"Would you like to make this the *frame of mind* you operate from on a daily basis?"

"Yes!"

"And suppose you used this way of thinking and feeling as your *intentional stance* in life? Does every part of you agree and support this?"

"Yes."

Aligning Attention With Higher Level Intentions

In order to *align* our attentions with our intentions, we have to go higher and first make our intentions explicit. Once we do that, then we can bring those intentions back down and set a new *attention* that will serve the higher frames. Since it is the nature of attention to come and go, it becomes our responsibility to align it with our highest intentions. When we do that, then at the *attentional level* we will notice, pay attention, go into sensory awareness, and focus on what will serve our intentions well. In the end, this will offer us more choices and potentials puts *attention at the service of intention.*

To do this, make sure you have *permission* to **live in the new attention** (the Permission Frame Game). That may mean permission to step out of your Comfort Zone so that you can allow the new intentions to become the higher level *attractors*. As you do, you give the higher executive frames an opportunity to become your self-organizing attractors. And because this will take time, give yourself permission also to take the time necessary to *intend your new attention*. (The Patience Game)

Intention of Intention Game
Living by an Intense Desired Outcome

Use the following exercise to set some new intentions and intentions-of-intentions to govern your healthy habits of eating and exercising right.   Use it to develop your "will power" without all of the stress and strain that has traditionally been connected with such. You can use this exercise by yourself or have someone coach your through the process. You can use it by simply thinking about some activity that you do, but not with the power and focus that you really want, or by thinking about some activity that you want to do, but seem to never get around to.

1) Identify what you want.

Start with your immediate goal. What do you want? Later you can run with on lots of other goals that fit into this general area: exercising, eating right, fitness, etc.   As you ask, "What do you want?" identify your first level intentions. Describe your desired outcome specifically.

> "What do you seek to experience, accomplish, feel, or create in life by means of the things you *think, feel, say, and do?*"

2) Identify your higher level "wants" — all the way up.

After the first set of outcomes, continue the same process:

> "What do you want from that want?"
> What do you seek to accomplish by achieving your first level intentions?"
> "Why do you want to go for such things?"
> "How will getting these things enrich your life?"
> "What will they do for you?"

Identify fully the desired outcomes of your desired outcomes. Continue this process until you begin to loop around the higher intentions or just repeat them in different words. When you do that, you have generally "reached the ceiling" of your constructions.

3) Diagram the structure of your intentions and intentions-of-intentions and compare them to your attentions.

To keep track of the every higher executive levels, use a circle for your *primary state* intentions and attentions. This will specify the first order things uppermost in your mind (intentions) and things "in the front of your mind" (attentions).   Then use a circle or a "frame" line to indicate each higher level of desired outcomes which set the higher frames of your life.

> "What do you *attend to* on a regular basis every day?"

4) Redesign your executive levels of intentional states.

When you have finished the elicitation and diagraming, step back into a witnessing and observing state. This will create the space so you can *Quality Control* the experience. "Run an ecology check" on these levels of mind that you have uncovered.

> Do they serve you well?
> Do they enhance your life?

Do they set the direction and orientation that you want your life to go in?

Do they empower you in bringing out your personal excellence?

If not, then redesign them by identifying and specifying what you do want.

Diagram 6:2

Intention

Intention

Intention
First level Intention or Goal

Person —>   Life Events

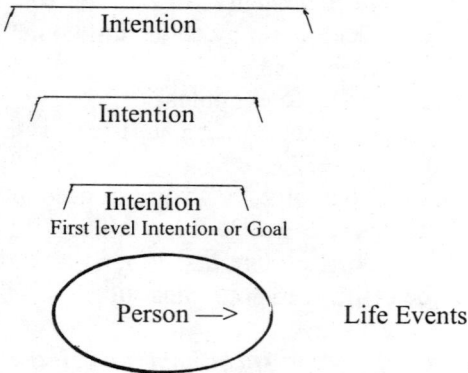

5) With a set of higher level intentions and intentions-of-intentions, set into your highest executive self to establish and install these as your Intentional Stance.

"As you consider these positive intentions and higher level positive outcomes, do you really want these for your life?" (Yes)

"Are you willing to let these govern your mind-and-emotions?" (Yes)

"Are you willing to accept the discomfort and unpleasantness of stepping outside of your old comfort zone and continually affirming and practicing these new intentions until they 'take' and become your executive intentional states?" (Yes)

"Is there any part of you that would object to letting these

higher frames rule and govern your life?" (No)
"So you really want these?" (Yes)
"No, I don't think you do!" (Yes I really, really do!)
"So go inside and make an agreement with your highest executive self to commission these frames to take over and become your Intentional Stance in life."

6) Future pace and reframe all objections.
"Does every part of your higher mind fully agree and align with this? Does any part of you object?"
If you get a yes to the objection question, then identify the objection.
"What's the objection or fear?"
"What part of me hesitations to take this intentional stance and let these higher positive outcomes govern my life?"
Frequently, it's just the dislike of being out in a new place, outside of the old comfort zone, and a sense of the unfamiliar. If there is an objection, dovetail the meaning of that objection into one of the intentional states. For example, suppose a part of your mind says, "I'm afraid that if I set fitness too high a value, I'll never have any fun or enjoy food again." Then ask,
"What *resource* would you need in order to enjoy food and have lots of fun as you pursue fitness?"
Build that resource into your intentional frame.
Future pace.
"Step into the higher intentional frames and imagine taking this as your attitude, motivation, understanding, intention as you move through the world tomorrow, next week, and in the months to come. Notice how this intention or these intentions transforms how you think, feel, and relate."
"And as you step into this higher positive intention, and the next intention-of-intention and experience this executive state fully and completely, and in just the way you find it most compelling and resourceful, imagine operating in your everyday life from this place... And just enjoy the transformation that occurs because of it. And don't you really want to be this way now and wouldn't you like this to become your *way of being in*

the world from this day forward? ..."

Summary

- The Intentional Stance is a great Game to play in life. It is the *Living Life on Purpose* Game.
- To truly *take charge* of our lives for personal excellence, flush out, detect, examine, and consciously choose your higher intentions.
- Mastery begins when we align our *attentions* with our higher level *intentions*.   Within every thought we think, we have both an attentional content or focus and an intentional design.   If we do not **intentionally** take charge of our attentions from a higher level, our attentions will drive us and often run us ragged. Conversely, when we take an Intentional Stance from our meta-outcomes, personal genius becomes easy.
- Flush out and stubbornly refuse (i.e., say *"No!"* to) some of the old intentions that have been set in your mind.   If these set you up for the Ease and Comfort Game, the Path of Lease Resistence Game, the Live it Up Now Game, then these will be the higher intentions that actually govern your attentions.

Now That You Know—Here's What To Do

- Make a list of your *Whys* regarding why you want to play a brand new Game with Food and Exercise. Why do you want that? How would that be valuable to you?
- Write out the higher *Whys of your Whys*. Why do you want that outcome?
- Once you have written out the higher *Whys* ... Write them out in a succinct and memorable way and post around your home and office.

OUR ABILITY TO PLAY
NEW GAMES IS DIRECTLY
RELATED TO
- OUR ABILITY TO SAY
"NO!" TO THE OLD
GAMES,
- "YES!" TO THE NEW
GAMES AND
- ACCESSING A GREAT
BIG WHY FOR DOING
THIS.

DO YOU HAVE YOUR
GREAT BIG WHY YET?

PART III:

USING YOUR POWERS
TO SAY *"NO!"*

Chapter 7

BECOMING AWARE

OF

OUR FOOD GAMES

If You are Eating for
All of the Wrong Reasons
Wrongly Motivated Eating will take on a Life of its Own

Games in This Chapter
The Psycho-Eating Game
The Neuro-Semantics of Eating Game
The Pleasure & Meta-Pleasure Game

If you do not have the fitness, health, vitality, energy, and body that you want (which is fully possible for you), then ... face it, you are playing some *Games* that just do not work and games that do not give you the *payoffs* you want. As you consider the Games you play with food, eating, snacking, exercising, staying active, etc., consider them in terms of the following results and benefits:

- Do they give you *the energy and vitality* so that you feel robust and enjoy a sense of vitality?
- Do they enable you to attain and maintain *the kind of body, weight, and shape* that you want?
- Do they give you the kind of *inner sense of control* so

that you don't fear food or fear of saying *"No"* to it?
- Do they put you in charge of your own fitness so that you *have* it rather than it *having* you?
- Do they give you the *pleasure, fun, and ecstasy* so that staying healthy, eating right, exercising regularly is "a piece of cake?"

Are you Aware of Your "Control?"

Over the years, I've worked with lots of people whose actions gave every evidence that they were "out-of-control" when it came to eating. While working on this program, I worked with one male friend in his mid-forties who described himself as a "fat slob" with "no self-control." When he said that, I responded by saying,

"Tom, that's incredible. You say you have been 'out-of-control?' What do you have to assume about yourself in order to be out-of-control with your eating and exercising?"

It took him back for a moment.

"Well, I have to assume that I *am* out-of-control and that *something* else is controlling me."

"Like aliens inhabiting your body and taking over your mind."

(Laughing) "Well, no... It's more like I just can't get myself to do what I want to do and know I should."

"So you tell your hands, 'Put down that chocolate cake!' But it rebels. 'Ha, ha! I'm going to make you eat this! Ha. Ha!'"

(Laughing) "That sounds so silly. ... but it's not like that. I see the dessert, for example, and just want to taste it..."

"Yes, that's the feeling of the yearning. A great feeling. But then how do you not *just have the feelings of the yearning* without being *forced* by some alien power be a slave to your hands grabbing it and forcing it down your throat? ... What else has to be true for you in order to experience food in such an out-of-control way?"

"Well, just that I'm not in the habit of telling myself 'No.'"

"And is that true? Do you just not tell yourself 'No?'"

"Yes, most of the time. I assume that if I want it that much that..." (pause).

"That what?"

"Well, I guess that I should eat it or that I deserve it."

"Thank God you only do this with the craving for food and not for sex or violence! ... Tom, you do say *'No!'* to those cravings when they are not fitting, don't you?"

"Of course!"

"Good, then there's no question you can tell yourself *'No!'* and follow through. Just checking."

PSYCHO-EATING —
Eating for all the Wrong Reasons

When we step back from food, it immediately becomes apparent that we should eat primarily *for fuel and energy* and not for comfort, fulfillment, reward, love, nurturing, validation, status, emotional stress, etc. That's eating for psychological reasons. It is psycho-eating. If we eat to deal with loneliness, boredom, anxiety, depression, anger, frustration, and any other of a hundred emotional states— then we are eating *for the wrong reasons.* That's why I always start out by asking,

"You ate what? You ate how much? What were you thinking?"

"Well, I didn't have anything else to do while the game was on and everybody else was munching on the junk food that we had out. It's what we always do when the Super Bowl is on."

"So what were you thinking about at the party?"

"Just that, hey, it's a party."

"And the meaning of that... is what?"

"It's time to eat up, to let go."

"Why?"

"To enjoy yourself."

"So let me see if I have this right. You were eating to be social, to party, to experience joy. Right?"

'Yes, that's right."

"So you were eating for all of the wrong reasons. No wonder you overdid it, experienced no sense of self-control, and were *played by the Game* rather than had mastery over your body and what you put into it! It makes sense. With frames like that, anybody would over-eat the wrong things."

Healthy Food Frames

Our bodies require fuel. That's obvious. So, to supply fuel, we eat. Actually, we must eat if we want energy, vitality, an active lifestyle, movement, and a healthy metabolism. And that's pretty much it.

When we add *psychology* to food (that is, the Frame Games that we play), we create a mix for some real problems, as the obesity statistics and dieting fads indicate. Anything other than this sets a frame about food that will not serve us well.

In terms of detecting the frame we use with regard to eating, answer the following set of questions:

- Why do you eat?
- Why do you eat *what* you eat?
- What significance does food hold for you?
- Is food important? How? In what way?
- What emotions drive you to eat?
- What emotions do you experience when you eat?
- What do you believe about your eating and weight?
- What do you believe about your ability to resist temptation?

There are so many unenhancing frames for eating. Apparently, we can (and do) attach a great many emotional values to the activity of eating. This typically began early in life when we were rewarded with desserts and treats, comforted with a bowl of soup, and spent time with loved ones eating. No wonder we can link up all kinds of psychological states to the experience of eating. It's so easy to attach massive pleasure to eating. When that happens, of course, then it becomes difficult to stop eating. Why "deprive" yourself of "pleasure?" Why "lose" out on comfort, fulfillment, reward, socializing, etc.?

What *references* do you have for eating? What *frames of mind* have you developed over the years about eating and dieting? What meanings have become incorporated in your *frameworks?* Out of these, what **Food Frame Games** do you play with eating and dieting? The Game of *Yo-Yo Up and Down the Scales*? *Now I'm Dieting/ Now I'm Not. If I Don't Notice the Cookies Hidden in the Socks Drawer, then I'm Not Really Eating Them. Ain't My Weight Awful?*

There's lots of food Frame Games that we can play. As with every

Frame Game, these often involve the beliefs that we've built about eating. Among these are the following:

- *I'm Out of Control With My Eating* Game.
- *I Can't Help It, It's My Genes!* (The Blame Game)
- *It's Useless and I'm Hopeless. I've Tried Everything and Nothing Works.* (The Despair Frame Game)
- *I Eat to Fill a Hole, a Void, an Emptiness.*
- *Other People Can Lose Weight, But I Can't.* (Helpless Game)
- *Keep Me Back From Myself!* (I put off eating as far as possible into the day, because once I get started, I won't stop eating. It's like letting a beast out of a cage.)
- *I Have a Sweet Tooth and Can't Help Myself.*
- *Just I Little of This Won't Hurt.* "It won't matter if I indulge just this once."
- *Tomorrow I Will Begin a New Diet and This Time I'm Going to Really Stick to It!*
- *I Have to Starve Myself to be Thin.*

The Neuro-Semantics of "Food" and Eating

If the *meaning* of food and of the experience of eating plays *that* much of a role in how we feel and act with regard to food, then it's time that we explore our own food semantics.

- What does "food" mean to you?
- What does "eating" mean to you?

To do this, let's engage in the following *thought experiment.* This comes from "The Pleasure and Meta-Pleasure Pattern" that we use in Meta-States training.

Step 1: Imagine a Food Pleasure

Take a moment now to recall an exquisite pleasure. While you could recall a good night of sleep, a restful afternoon on a sunny beach, the organismic pleasure of sexual stimulation, the warmth of a hot bath, the relaxation of the muscles, the smell of a bubble bath. etc. I want you to consider *the pleasure of food,* the tastes and smells of a culinary dish that brings lot of delight to you. Pick a pleasure of food and fully notice the smell, taste, and look of a tender, juicy steak; or a tasty, tart glass of fresh orange juice; etc.

Re-access the experience completely and fully so that you feel the pleasure in a strong and full way, then anchor it in your experience by attaching a sight, sound, or sensation.

How is it pleasurable to you?

Step 2: Explore the Meta-Levels of Pleasure

As you are noticing and experiencing that pleasure, answer the following questions:

What about it gives you pleasure?
Why do you find it significant and important?
What is the meaning of this experience to you?
How do you find this activity valuable?
What does this pleasure mean about yourself?
What does it do for you?

Keep asking these questions of meaning in order to discover what meanings you give to eating and drinking. Begin with the first layer of meanings that you give to it. After that, take each of those meta-pleasures and ask the same questions about it until you move up higher and higher with regard to the frames you have put around the experience.

The Structure of Pleasure

It's easy to experience basic *pleasure.* We only need to use our sensory equipment of our eyes, ears, nose, and skin to experience something. If, however, we want to experience *happiness,* we have to bring mind and meaning to the experience and set frames of significance about something. Doing that transforms the primary pleasure into a meta-level pleasure, or happiness. It makes the experience *much more than it is.* By adding layer upon layer of rich meanings, it becomes semantically loaded. In this way, we transform simple experiences of eating, drinking, exercising, relaxing, etc. into addictions, compulsions, disorders, etc.

Happiness does not result from having more and more primary level experiences of pleasure. It results from developing *more ability to appreciate*, to see value, to endow with meaning, to give more importance and significance to something. The more significance we give to an experience—the more pleasant and enjoyable we make it in our neurology.

Primary pleasures feel good mostly because it stimulates our body's sense receptors. So when it comes to sensory pleasures, we do not merely eat, we rather find pleasure in a thousand combinations of flavors, textures, and temperatures in a multitude of foods. We develop appetites for countless combinations of foods, smells, tastes, sights, sounds, etc.

From primary pleasures we feel stimulated, gratified, healthy, etc. It induces a feeling of being alive. No wonder we like it! This invigorates us for more and serves as the foundation for motivation. Our nervous system uses pleasures as a reward system for behaviors that enrich our survival.

At the primary level, pleasure takes no effort. At this level, it happens in an effortless way. We experience a sight, sound, sensation, smell, or taste and don't have to try to like it, it just feels good.

Yet there is a surprising quality to primary pleasures. *We can get too much of them.* They have thresholds. When they cross a threshold, what we experienced as pleasure, now becomes pain. When the warm sun on our skin becomes too much, we burn. Too much time in a hot tub, we wrinkle, then we may feel sick and even faint. Too many chocolate chip cookies and we feel sick also and then hate ourselves for over-eating. Normally, we do not over-indulge in sensory based pleasures because they reach a threshold level that turns the pleasure into a dis-pleasure or even a painful experience.

This thresholding of primary level pleasures also speaks about the evanescent nature of such pleasures. They can *vanish* very quickly. In fact, just as soon as we try to understand the pleasure, *Poof!* it disappears. Typically, bringing the "mind" to analyze pleasure causes it to vanish.

There's a *time-limit quality* to primary pleasures. They only last for a short period of time. Compare your own sense of pleasure of food from when you begin to sit down and enjoy a meal to those moments afterwards when you feel full. Do you want to keep eating? Probably not. You feel full. The sensory deprivation has been fulfilled and no longer idles ... waiting for stimulation. Now you feel satiated.

Primary pleasures are a here-and-now phenomena, a present-moment experience, it exists in *this* moment, and does not extend out very far into the future.

Our primary pleasures operate by our sense receptors in a passive way. This gives them a primitive and neurological basis. Typically we experience them apart from cognition. We experience them in more of a pre-cognitive way. *Mindlessness*, in fact, sometimes helps us with "just experiencing" the pleasure purely and simply.

Fritz Perls' recommended that we "lose our mind and come to our senses." To do this we have to "stop the world," that is, the world of "mind" and language, the conceptual world of higher level abstractions. We stop *that* world in order to re-experience the sensory-based world.

All primary level pleasures lose their luster after awhile. This happens because we have sensory thresholds. And because sensory pleasures threshold, we find that we can (and do) become bored with everything. Not only does too much of any pleasure threshold, but even *too regular a diet of a particular pleasure* gets old which leaves us with a tendency to lose appreciation for it.

Because primary level pleasure works this way, it can makes things seem strange and confusing. What we once wanted so much and thought that we would never tire of—we tire of. In fact, we normally do become tired of pleasures. The pleasure begins at a high pitch of desire and then it runs down.

By themselves, sensory based pleasures are non-addictive. Pleasures do not become addictive at that level because of the built-in threshold. When we get too much touch—it begins to chafe and hurt. Too much sun creates a burning. Eat too much and we experience heartburn, stomach ache, and discomfort. "I feel like I'm going to burst."

Now imagine that we return to this level of experience and eat at this level. If we were to do so, we would not find food addictive.

Higher Level Pleasures

The pleasures of meaning, significance, and importance that we create at a higher level *about* the primary level pleasure of food operates in a very different way from primary pleasure. When we move up the levels, we set frames of meaning and that moves us into the realm of our neuro-semantics. We move to this place as we bring thoughts-and-emotions of *value, delight, pleasure, importance, significance, etc.* to the primary experience.

At this level, food is no longer just "food." At least, we do not experience it as just food. It now becomes "comfort," "fulfillment," "sense of being rewarded," "being social," being "cool," feeling "loved and valued," important, etc. Here we eat for higher reasons, but for all of the wrong reasons.

- What does food or eating signify for you?
- What meanings do you give to eating?
- What memories are linked to eating, to desert, to fast foods, etc.?

Pleasure at the semantic levels causes considerable change to our experience. New characteristics emerge. What distinguishes pleasure at these two different levels?

In happiness we have a sense that we *"have"* the pleasure rather than the pleasure *"has"* us. This contrasts with the passive receptivity of pleasure. In happiness we experience a sense of being in charge. That's how people can "feel" a sense of "control" by over-eating, abusing alcohol, etc.

At the higher level, happiness involves "mind," a defining and reality creating consciousness. By bringing "mind" to a primary pleasure, we can transform food, eating, even vomiting, starving oneself, etc. into meaning all kinds of things: control, power, love, feminity, masculinity, etc. This explains why some people can find *the strangest things enjoyable.*

Personally, I don't understand how trudging through snow, facing sixty mile an hour winds, forty-degrees below zero cold, and needing to use oxygen masks to climb the world's tallest mountains "fun." My neurology doesn't call that "pleasurable." My neurology hasn't *learned* to do that. But some people have. They find it "fun"—they experience it as wild and wonderful fun. They have taught their neurology to actually experience that as "fun." It's now in their muscles.

Nor does my neuro-linguistics move me to join a Polar Bear Club.

Freezing my rear-end in ice-water just doesn't "make sense" to me(!), which explains why I haven't done it and have no plans to do it.

I do go for cross-country skiing in the high country and sometimes I do so for eight hours at a time, and have lots of "fun." I can read in front of a warm fireplace in a mountain cabin and call that fun. Yet I know friends whose neuro-semantics would experience "reading" as a chore, a pain, a bother, as everything but enjoyable.

I don't find pleasure in living on a starvation diet. Nor do I find it fun stuffing myself. Yet some people do. Such "fun" does *not* occur mostly at the primary level, but at the higher levels of one's *frames of meaning*. The pleasure we *give* to eating occurs due to the investment of meaning that we attribute.

What foods do you like and "can't help yourself from eating?" You experience it in that way because of the meanings, memories, and other frames of mind that you bring to it. It all makes sense. It just may not be healthy or appropriate. This explains how we may experience the same food as addictive and obnoxious. Our learning histories and value systems can create *a higher level of pleasure* that can completely over-ride the primary level.

Figure 7: 1

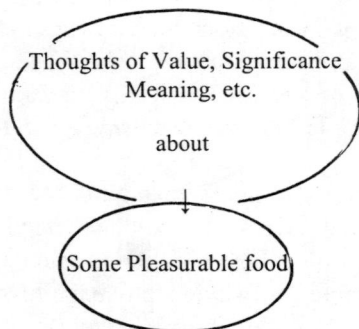

Thoughts of Value, Significance
Meaning, etc.

about

Some Pleasurable food

"Good food," then, as beauty and fun, lies in the "eye of the beholder" or more accurate, in the "mind" of the neuro-semantic evaluator. This realization makes us all unique in our pleasuring-of-pleasure. It also explains how a pleasure can last so long. Unlike primary pleasure that's mainly in the here-and-now, meta-pleasures can last and last. We may not even recognize the pleasure until we create it — at some later time. We later look back on an experience and then give it meaning and value. Then we say, "My, didn't we have fun doing that?"

In this way we can *learn* to enjoy things that have no inherent pleasure. This explains how some people can become sadists. It explains how others can "enjoy" masochistic experiences —they have coded it as significant, meaning, and important.

Cognitive psychologist, Csikszentmihalyi (1991) in *"Flow"* described the phenomenology of enjoyment in terms of investment of psychic energy. Enjoyment occurs when we invest our consciousness totally and completely so that attention becomes focused like a laser beam on something of value. The meta-pleasure comes from "a heightened sense of control" and especially from the sense of exercising control — or running our own brains.

"As our studies have suggested, the phenomenology of enjoyment has eight major components. When people reflect on how it feels when their experience is most positive, they mention at least one, and often all, of the following."

"First, the experience usually occurs when we confront *tasks we have a chance of completing.* [Context which it occurs.] Second, we must be able to *concentrate* on what we are doing. [State needed.] Third and fourth, the concentration is usually possible because the task undertaken has *clear goals* and provides *immediate feedback.* [Driven by desired outcome and feedback.] Fifth, one acts with *a deep, but effortless involvement* that removes from awareness the worries and frustrations of everyday life. [Total focus.] Sixth, enjoyable experiences allow people to exercise *a sense of control* over their actions. [Meta-state of self-control.] Seventh, *concern for the self disappears,* yet paradoxically the sense of self emerges stronger after the flow experience is over. [Experience enriches semantics of self.] Finally, *the sense of the duration of time is altered;* hours pass by in minutes, and minutes can stretch out to seem like hours. [Time distortion.] The combination of all these elements causes a sense of deep enjoyment that is so rewarding people feel that expending a great deal of energy is worthwhile simply to be able to feel it." (p. 49)

The Pleasure of Meaning

What we find pleasurable from a higher level depends entirely upon our semantics, that is, how we attribute meaning and value to something. As we treat a primary pleasure like food as having very high psychological value, it becomes the neuro-semantics of that experience. That is, *the meaning gets into our neurology.* That's why we don't have to think about food having this or that meaning, it's programmed into our body.

Then our frames drive our neuro-semantic responses. Then we experience our *"drives"* for food, drink, eating, comfort, etc. as part of our identity (who we are), our destiny (I can't control it), and our values and motivations (I just feel driven to do this). .

From Pleasure to Addiction

This description of pleasure at primary and meta levels gives us a model for understanding "addiction" phenomena.

> **We can over-load a pleasure with too much meaning. And whenever we do *over-load* a basic pleasure with too much meaning, we create an "addiction."**

Food (or whatever) then becomes too meaningful, too significant, and too loaded with "pleasure" — and so begins to effect mind-and-emotions in "addictive" ways. Mentally we *obsess* about the object of our pleasuring — and emotionally/ behaviorally we *act and feel compulsively* about it.

William Glasser (1976, *Positive Addiction*) further distinguishes addictions (as those activities and experiences that we have over-loaded with meaning and pleasure) into *positive* and *negative* addictions.

Negative Addiction:

Does the "addiction" leave one worn out, depleted of energy, less functional, less resourceful, less able to carry on life's everyday activities of work, relationship, exercise, etc.?

Positive Addiction:

Does the "addiction" leave one built up, renewed, rejuvenated, more energetic, creative, resourceful, flexible, alert, insightful, etc. and more able to bring these resources into the way the person relates, works, plays, etc?

The Structure of Your Food Addiction

In summary, here is the pattern for discovering the meta pleasures that you have attached to food to over-load it in importance. First we need to discover where and how we have over-loaded a sensory pleasure with *too much enjoyment.* How have we set it up so that food means *too much* to us?

This explains why our *neuro-semantics* (meanings incorporated into our neurology) can get out of balance through attributing too *much meaning* to certain behaviors and use them to trigger for us "happiness." Yet in the long run we have to pay the price in various forms of unhappiness, misery and poor health.

The following represents the happiness pattern applied to over-used pleasures of food and pleasures that we wish did **not** give us so much delight. It enables us to look at the things that we no longer want to trigger the old Frame Games.

1) Identify the primary pleasure that means too much.

Menu list: chocolate cake, french fries, milk shake, etc.

2) Discover your frames driving the food pleasure

What positive meaning of value and significance do I give to this pleasure?

How is that important to you?

What pleasure do you get from that?

Get a list of 4 or 5 of the most important values that you have for that pleasure.

Diagram of the meta-levels of meanings about that pleasure, draw a circle designating your primary pleasure with each answer to this question as a higher frame of meaning and feeling *about* that pleasure.

3) Discover your Frames of Frames.

Repeat the same question for each response and move up the levels until you flush out all of the higher-level pleasurable meanings that you give to the food pleasure.

Sketch out the full structure of pleasure at all of its levels.

4) Sit back and appreciate the overall structure.

Take a moment to just notice, without any judgments, all of the meanings, values, beliefs, etc. that you generate *about* that initial primary food pleasure. Allow yourself to recognize that these meanings (semantics) *drive* your pleasure. They give it its meaning, energy, motivation, and power. Now you know **why** it "holds so much meaning for you."

5) Use your highest pleasuring.

Go to your highest meta-pleasure frame, access it fully and completely by stepping into it and "being there" now. As you do, allow yourself to become fully aware of these meaning of pleasure and just imagine fully taking this perceptual frame of mind into some other everyday activities, because you can...

And I wonder what other everyday sensory-based activities can you creatively imagine using to trigger this high level frame of mind? What if you felt this fully when you were walking, taking the stairs, saying "no" to fatty foods, etc.? Imagine fully being in this state in some particular context doing something that typically tempts you to over-eat, and suppose you had this state fully and completely, in just the way you want it... now notice just how this will transform your experience.

6) De-Meaning/De-Enjoy.

Put your hand over the diagram of the sets of higher frames of meanings about eating and ask yourself: If I took away this set of frames about the pleasure, *how much would that reduce my enjoyment?*

Continue to do this until you get a sense of which meanings you need to eliminate in order to reduce the power of this pleasure. How many of the meanings do I need to take away before it starts to exist as just whatever it "is" at the primary level— eating for health and nutrition rather than for comfort, to de-stress anger, to overcome loneliness, etc.?

Figure 7:2:

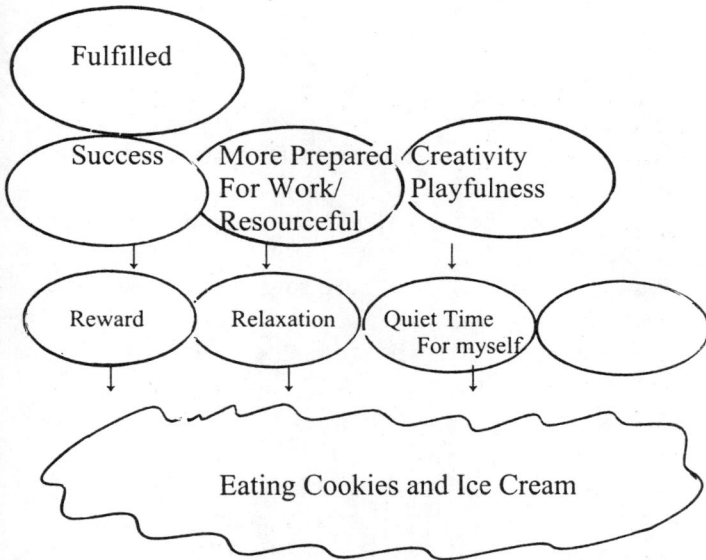

7) *Put this new program out into your future*

Imagine yourself fully engaged in the primary pleasure of eating. When fully and honestly in that imagination, hear yourself say,

"This is *just* food. It nourishes my body—a nice pleasure for the moment, but no more. It *just* provides fuel. I refuse to over-load it with meaning. If I love it too much — I see globs of ugly fat growing at my mid-section" (attach whatever *dis*pleasure that works for you!).

8) Access your highest meta-pleasure frames fully.

Allow yourself to step into that highest level meaning and to be there completely and fully. As you step fully into this state and experience it fully then *realize fully* that you can do so without needing to engage in that behavior anymore. Now allow your creative part to identify other behaviors that you can do that will allow you to experience this meta-level meaning in everyday life.

Summary

- There you have it. Now you know *why* and *how* you have attached far too much meaning to food and to eating. Now you know.
- Now decide. Giving it *that* much meaning—does that serve you well? Does that enhance your fitness or the way you look? Do you need to give food that much meaning?
- Take charge. Okay, who's going to be the boss— you or the food? The program to eat and eat and eat, and to eat all the wrong stuff makes perfect sense given the meaning frames you've attached to it. But it's just a frame of reference, just a map and not the territory.
- Are you ready to play a brand new frame Game with food? How about "Hey, it's just fuel!" Frame Game?
- Are you ready to say "Hell No!" so some of the old Frame Games that you've played with food, like the compulsive Frame Game, "I've got to eat you!"

Now That You Know—Here's What To Do

- Do you *psycho-eat*? Make a list of all of the Psychological reasons that you over-eat or misuse food.
- What *pleasures* have been attached to food whether during childhood or over the years of your adult life? Has food become too loaded with meaning and pleasure? Do you need to de-pleasure it so that it can

become just food again?

- Try on the words, "It's just food ... I refuse to overload it with psychological meanings and pleasures." Use this as a mantra during your meals this week.

PSYCHO-EATING

IS THAT THE "FAT" THAT'S BEEN IN MY HEAD? IS THAT THE FAT THAT HAS PREVENTED ME FROM TAKING CHARGE OF MY EATING AND THEREFORE WEIGHT?

COULD IT BE AS SIMPLE AS THAT?

HAVE I OVER-LOADED FOOD AND EATING WITH MEANINGS THAT THEY CANNOT BEAR?

WHAT MEANINGS HAVE I GIVE TO FOOD?

AM I READY TO LET FOOD BE FOOD, TO LET IT BE FUEL FOR MY BODY AND TO FIRE FOOD FROM BEING MY THERAPIST?

Old
Eating & Food Frame Games

Do you *now know* the Games you've been playing? If not, go back to chapter one and start over! Really. Why? Because *detection* is truly the beginning place. First we detect Frame Games. Only when we know what we're up against can we intelligently transform it.

Check all of the Games that you've been playing and write out any food or eating Games that you've been playing that I don't have listed here. *Awareness* may not always be curative *per se,* but it is the beginning place for empowering transformations.

Psycho-Eating Games

"I eat when I'm tired, lonely, bored, frustrated, stressed, happy, etc." Game (The Emotional Eating Game)

"I use food as a Friend, Therapist, etc." Game

"Food is a Mechanism for Coping with Feelings" Game

"I have to eat when I feel anxious, nervous, like a failure, etc." Game

Blaming *Games*

"If It weren't for my mother" (father, teachers, husband, etc.) Game

"If it weren't for the commercials, for the restaurants making the food so appealing."

"I Shouldn't have to do all this work in order to be thin. It's unfair." (The Peevishness Game)

"The doctors, diet programs, media, etc. are out to get me, to sucker me into the latest fad." (The Paranoid Game)

Fear Games

"What if they laugh at you?" Game

"Making Mistakes is Terrible, therefore always cover your butt" Game

Excuse Games:

"Fat is a genetic thing; I can't make any difference in my

weight, fitness, or health" Game.

"I've tried and it just doesn't make much difference" Game

"I have tried so hard, but nothing ever really works."

"I can't feel a sense of relief or comfort without some food."

"There's too much to do, I can't juggle everything."

Discounting Games

"It's just calories anyway" Game.

"I'm responsible for everything, that's why I eat as I do. I have to de-stress."

"I feel so responsible for the messes that others get into and then need to eat to calm myself."

Waiting to Start Games

"If only I could find an easy program" Game

"I wish I could find a diet that would really work." (The Wishing Game)

The Helpless Games

"You Can't Really Change Anything."

"I'm a Victim of my genetics, family, upbringing, etc."

"I'm Powerless to Change my weight, my eating habits, my exercising habits, etc."

"Oh, God, another day of eating in an out-of-control way!"

Chapter 8

FRAME GAMES

FOR WEIGHT CONTROL

THAT JUST DON'T WORK

"But I'm doing this to control my Weight!"
"Good, does it work?"
"Well, no."
"Great! Are you now ready to try something that will?"

Games in This Chapter
The Judgment Game
The Self-Contempt Game
The "Hate all Fat" Game
The "I need the latest diet, program" Game
The "Path of Lease Resistence and Ease at all Costs" Game
The Impatience Game

Discovering *how and why* you eat the way you do puts *the key to transformation* in your hands. As a meaning maker and a frame setter, you can play a whole new Game—if you want to. It then puts choice into your hands.

And in that choice, you may first have to *find and refuse* those current

Frame Games that have arisen from your frames about eating. That's the purpose of this chapter. Let's identify some of the Games that people commonly attempt to play in controlling their weight, but which are Games that just do not work. Do you know them yet? Would you like to?

There are many *non-working* Games that surround our relationship to eating and exercising which are not workable or sustainable. Crash diets, starvation diets, counting calories, eliminating all meat, eliminating all carbohydrates, investing in the latest exercise equipment, etc. are but a few examples of *Frame Games* that don't cut it.

Why not?

What's wrong with most programs for health and fitness?

Even though we have become increasingly conscious of our bodies in terms of health, good eating habits, etc., the disturbing paradox is that more people seem to be struggling with getting fat, becoming overweight, and experience less fitness and health.

The Judgment Game

Lots of people play *the Judgment Game* in an attempt to judge themselves into doing what's right with regard to food and exercise. Have you ever played that one? Has it ever really helped? Does it succeed in the long run? It doesn't work, does it? "Judging" yourself in a harsh way by name-calling, insulting, and threatening may put the pressure on and temporarily get you off your butt. But more often than not, all of the negative emotions that you evoke by doing so will only work for the short term, and double back on you in the long run.

"I'm nothing but a fat slob! Get off your big fat butt, will you?!"

Do you ever play the Judgment Game with yourself? Or, worse, with someone else? To play the Judgment Game, begin from the state of displeasure, dislike, and anger. Then as you assume the role of a Judge, begin to think in terms of harsh judgments and how you need to put the violator in his or her place. When you begin to make your pronouncements, use a harsh and ugly tone of voice, lean down from the lofty bench, and point your mental finger. Now, tell yourself in a demanding and insulting way what you "have to do."

Judgments doesn't always occur in so explicit a form. Judgments can also be very subtle and, like everything else, can habitualize so that we don't even notice them. It can therefore become most insightful to begin to become aware of the Judgment Game you may be playing with yourself. So, as you begin to listen in to the internal critic that chatters away in your head, begin to notice the statements, opinions, recommendations, suggestions, etc. that go flying through your head —and think about them in terms of the *judgments* you make. Surprise yourself. Take a day and begin to count the number of judgments in that day just for the sake of discovering how prone to judgment you may be.

We can even play the judgment Game and not notice. The "judgments" may not seem like *judgments,* but as "realistic comments," motivational statements trying to get us to eat better, etc. Listen to your own self-talk: any conflict going on, ordering, bullying, harsh statements, demands, awfulizing, insults?

How many *judgments* do you make in an average day?

How much of your internal chatter involves judging??

What are the forms of judgment that you typically use?

Any an internal fight with yourself?

Do you feel bullied by your demands?

Do your judgments confuse *you* with your *behaviors?*

Do your judgments interfere with your self of personal dignity?

Do you go into a protective or defensive mode when it comes to eating or exercising?

Do you trust yourself and feel confident that you can get yourself to act on your goals?

Some people play the judgment and experience is a continuous high-pitched shrieking in their head insulting and degrading themselves. Others only experience it as a sense of "wrongness," or "incompetence," or "distrust in self."

The best solution for *the Judgment Frame Game* is the *Acceptance Game* which we will learn to play in a later chapter. For some, shifting from judgment to acceptance will be a big shift. So to facilitate that transition, and just for a moment of sanity, let's de-commission the old Judgment Game so that you can have a quieter internal world. That will make learning easier and more permanent as well.

A MOMENT OF SANITY
De-Commissioning the Judgment Game

Suppose you have become a veteran player of the Judgment Game? What can you do about it? Several things:

1) Become aware of the Game of Judgment.

First just become aware of it so that you can name it. "Ah, there I go! Defaulting to the Judgment Game!" Because compulsions typically involve unthinking behavior, permission to play the *Awareness Game* empowers us to catch ourselves and then choice. Awareness expands our consciousness. We develop a sense of our self-watching self. This expands perception.

2) Dis-identify from the judgment.

It's just a judgment. And to make a "judgment," things have to be compared, and someone has to make the comparison and use some set of criteria as standards. You are more than whatever judgment you or another have made about you. Shift to begin playing the "I am more than what I eat" Game!

3) Center Yourself in Your Own Innate Worth

Identify yourself as a growing, developing, and learning person who has worth and value as a member of the human race. You don't have to earn it; it's a given. Center yourself in that thought. You are more than your body, your thoughts, your emotions, your behaviors, your speech. These functions are just that, *functions.* You express yourself by thinking, emoting, speaking and behaving.

Absolutely refuse any and all *conditional* judgments: "if you do this, you will be a somebody, "when you do this, people will love you," "until you lose so many pounds, nobody will want you..."

4) Fully Explore the Judgment.

Who has made the judgment? When? Where? About what? Using what criteria? Is the judgment valid or invalid? To what degree? How much of it has some validity? What is the quality and nature of the judgment: kind or harsh, helpful or hurting, personal or impersonal, etc.? After you have explored the judgment, decide how much of it could be useful information to you and what you want to do about it.

5) *Reformulate the Judgment.*

Restate the judgment in a kind and considerate way so that you feel validated and affirmed as you take the information and transform it into useful data that you can use to enhance your life. How can I reformulate the judgment so that it gives me valued instructions about what to specifically do that will enhance my life?

6) *Practice just Describing.*

To talk without judgment means learning how to describe in sensory based terms and eliminating the evaluative terms. In this way we can say almost anything to ourselves or another without giving offense or insult. Adopt a matter-of-fact tonality as you would say something like, "The sky is blue.... " Now, using *that* tonality, say, "I have gained some weight and size in my thighs..." Practice screening out all emotion-laden terms as you just describe things.

7) *Reduce all Gesture and Tones of Judgment.*

Once you have reduced the language of judgment and turned evaluations into sensory-based descriptions, refine all of the other gestures, tones, movements, etc. of "judgment" so that you not only *speak non-judgmentally,* but also *sound and gesture* without judgment. This means no pointing finger, tonality of judgment, etc. Practice playing this Game with yourself while talking to people. At first just watch your body as it speaks with judgment. Then begin to adjust it so as to reduce such gestures.

8) *Use Counter-Judging to Judge all your Judging*

As you catch and identify the judgment words, sounds, gestures, etc., judge the judgment as not necessary, useless, worthless, ineffective, disgusting, etc.

The Self-Contempt Game

There's another Game in town that's pretty popular among those who *want* to lose weight and who indeed *try* to lose weight. Like the

Judgment Game, people use it to get themselves to take action and to get off their butts. But it doesn't work, at least not for long. This Game involves a judgment as well, and yet it elicits something else, something different from mere judgment. It evokes contempt. Disgust. This is the *"I'm so Hopeless and Helpless"* Frame Game.

By *contempting* oneself, lots of people think that by giving themselves a good dose of self-hatred, this will get them off their fat, good-for-nothing butts and get them to stop eating like a pig. They actually talk this way. I've heard them. I've even seen such in writing in journals.

Yet this hardly ever works. And when it does, it tends to only work for the short term. It never lasts.

What explains this ineffectiveness? Several things. First, playing the Game of Self-Contempt leaves one in a state of intense negative feelings and those feelings will eventually undermine any positive direction that one sets. It also can leave one operating inside of a frame of self-contempt. That can lead to contempting and discounting good things.

A much better approach is the Frame Game of *Self-Dignity and Value.* Fitness, health, and weight management seems to work a lot better if we operate out of a state of self-acceptance and personal dignity. Then we eat right and exercise properly because we have a frame of mind of respect for ourselves, our bodies, and our health.

It takes that kind of a mind-set in order to truly be gentle with your body—with your thighs, your breasts, legs, stomach, skin, etc. Would you eat that way if you fully and completely *loved* yourself? More change will occur via love then by deprivation and force. If you're looking with critical eyes at yourself, then there's no such thing as an acceptable body. And messages of contempt, dislike, non-acceptance, and judgment will interfere with the art of being able to take effective action in eating and exercising.

Imagine your "ideal body" as lying out in your future, imagine it fully and completely in a way that's both realistic and compelling, and then, with that in mind, imagine taking your first step toward it today. How do you imagine yourself beginning to feel when you operate with that frame of mind? Wouldn't that be a much more productive Game to play? If you really want to live well in terms of your health habits, then be sure to nourish yourself in your self-attitude. How have you been nourishing yourself today? Have you been using the kind of attitude (frame of mind) that allows you to play a Game of respect, honor, dignity, and self-value?

"I Totally and Absolutely Hate Fat" **Frame Game**

This Game goes right along the same line as the Self-Contempt Frame Game. Many people play it because somehow they have the idea that if they could only raise their level of contempt and hatred of "fat" itself, that would get them into a more positive mode and get them to eat right. Yet like other Games of hate and judgment, it hardly ever works out that way.

I once saw a girl in therapy who wrote the following in her diary:
"I absolutely hate the idea of being fat; if I ever got fat, that would have to be the ultimate failure. If I became fat, that would negate anything and everything else I would accomplish. Nothing would matter if that happened."

It will probably will not surprise you that by the time her doctor sent her to me, she had an eating disorder. She wouldn't eat. And when she was forced to eat, she'd vomit it out. At just twenty-three her teeth were beginning to rot. And she looked terrible. All she sorted for was "fat." It was her worst nightmare. And her hatred of fat had created our internal intolerance of it which drove her to violate her health, peace of mind, and relationships.

"I Need the Latest Dieting Program" **Game**

Generally, any program for better management of eating and exercising that makes us *dependent* upon the program, specialized equipment, the secret formula about what you can and cannot eat, etc., only invites us to play *the wrong Game*. Such programs invite us to play a Game of Dependency. The Game essentially gets us into a frame of mind wherein we think:
"I can't really do it on my own. I need X, Y, and Z in order to lose weight, trim up, stay on a program."

This way of thinking undermines our powers rather than empowers. Diets fail for this reason. Instead of accepting, appreciating, and listening to our body for guidance, we follow some an external program that may or may not fit our needs or lifestyle. The diet tells us what we can and cannot eat. And more often than not, it makes us even more conscious of food and of what we cannot eat.

All of these Frame Games invite us to *distrust* ourselves, our bodies, our minds, our abilities to understand, our ability to get ourselves to do what's right for vigorous health, our ability to find the resources and to build the kind of states so that being disciplined becomes a way of life.

Accordingly you will find within most of the dieting programs ideas which—

- Discount *"will"* and especially "will power" (as if making an informed choice and following through was a bad thing!).
- Discount the importance and value of *"discipline"* (again, as if learning was a bad thing; something to stay away from).
- Discount and reduce any call to *effort, application, and mastery.*

What gives with all of this?

Ah, the presence of yet another toxic Frame Game that will undermine your personal resourcefulness.

"If Only I Could Find an Easy Way..." Game

A particular pernicious and toxic Frame Game involves a basic orientation in life for "the path of least resistance," "the path of ease and comfort," and "the path to immediate success." Play that Game and you're guaranteed to collect some grievances, upsets, and frustrations on a daily basis. Let that Game play you and you'll be a sucker for every new diet, every new exercise fad, every new video, every new whatever. You'll go for products that promise to "burn off fat while you sleep," "lose weight by sitting," etc.

Without question, the Game of wanting what you want *now* and with *ease and comfort* is a particularly seductive Game. It hooks thousands of us daily, and drags us by the nose to whatever product that someone happens to be hawking that day.

Yet how many who have attained mastery of mind-and-body do so without effort, energy, thought, and devotion? The pernicious nature of this *Frame Game* says, "Hey, you are not aiming for the body of an Olympic athlete so lighten up. Don't be so demanding on yourself." The illusion is that only the highest level of mastery calls for effort, energy, thought and devotion. Anything else does not.

When a person operates from the frame of mind that looks for and wants a path of ease and comfort, every effort, struggle, and investment seems like and feels like something "hard." This frame then views anything "hard" as "not fun."

Now you know the reason I have not written down, trying to simplify everything to a seventh grade level. The very passion for "dumbing down" arises from this same basic *sick* life orientation,

"Just hand everything to me on a silver plate." "Would you please spoon-feed me your great ideas. It's too much hard work to think."

Yet that violates a basic principle of learning. If we do not *take* in (ingest), chew over, digest, and incorporate as ours, a learning doesn't stick. Without that kind of engagement and encounter, the learning does become integrated and owned.

Most dieters who suffer or have suffered from the yo-yo effect of dieting suffer from impatience. They want the weight off *next week*! It doesn't work that way. Effective weight loss involves a slow and gradual process that allows the body to adjust its processes. Impatience and unrealistic expectations make for disappointment, frustration, and being thrown into a tailspin.

Summary

- Some food Frame Games just do not work. They may be rightly motivated, good intentioned, but in the end, *they do not work.* Rejoice every time you spot one of them knowing that you don't have to waste time with that ineffective Game any longer.
- Some eating Frame Games go about things in *all the wrong ways.* This is especially true of the Games of blaming, judging, shaming, insulting, etc. They may get you off your fat butt and get you started, but after

you're on the pathway, you stop playing. They sabotage your long term success.

Now That You Know—Here's What To Do

- What Games have you've played in an attempt to control your eating that have not worked?   ]
- Which Games mentioned in this chapter do you need to refuse to use?

THANK GOD,
I NOW KNOW WHAT DOESN'T WORK!

THE UNSANITY FORMULA:

TO KEEP DOING
WHAT YOU'VE DONE,
HOPING TO GET
A DIFFERENT RESULT
FROM WHAT
YOU'VE ALWAYS GOTTEN.

ARE YOU READY TO GIVE YOURSELF
A CHANCE TO DO SOMETHING
THAT MIGHT WORK?

-133-

Chapter 9

SLAYING & TAMING
THE DRAGONS
OF STUPIDITY

"When you think or act that way, does it help?"
"No, not really."
"Has it ever occurred to you to just **Stop it!?"**
"You mean I can?"

Games in This Chapter
"I am my Weight" Game
"I have no Control" Game
"Yes, Butt..." Game
Excuse Blow Out Game
Fear of Being Slim Game
Reversing Your Mind Game

Some Frame Games that we play regarding food and eating are so toxic, so morbid, so destructive, and so sick, that we simply need to recognize this about them, and *totally refuse* them. These Games differ from those of the previous chapter. However ineffective or confused those Games were, at least they sought to help us, albeit in all the wrong ways. Here I want to flush out those Games that are utterly stupid and that make life a living hell. *Thought viruses* drive and inform these Frame Games. If you set these as frames in your mind, they will become like *dragons* to you, breathing fire and devastating the landscape of your consciousness.

What's a person to do?

Learn the art of dragon slaying and dragon taming. Here we will learn how to refuse these Games entirely, to slay some of them and to tame some of them.

Using the Power Frame Games

In Chapters three and four we described how to play some frame Games that would enable us to claim, or reclaim, our personal powers. I hope that you have been continuing to play and practice those Power Zone Games. If you have, then you'll find it a "piece of cake" to now say *"Yes!"* to the Frame Games that will support you and a strong definitive *"No!"* to those that are toxic.

These Yes/No expressions give voice to our ability to choose, to forge a new path, to allow and permit, to set boundaries and limits, to welcome and embrace, and to refuse and disclaim. Daily practice will enable you to become more and more skilled at playing *"Accessing My Power Zone" Frame Game* and that will, in turn, truly empower you to decide which Games you'll play and which ones you'll resist, which ones you'll temper and which ones you'll set boundaries against. If you need to review chapters three and four, go and do so. Then meet us back here. If you have powered up and ready to go. Then, on to the dragons.

The Identification Frame Game
"I Am What I Eat"

Here's a Frame Game that will create real dragon state. It's a sick one too. Lots of people play the Game that they *are* what they eat or that they *are* what they look like. They say things to themselves like, "I'm just a fat slob."

We call this *identification*—they have *identified* (or over-identified) with a certain facet of their experience. This means that they use their body shape, size, weight, or their eating habits, likes, styles, etc. as an intimate part of their *self-definition.* As they experience, so they "are."

Identification, in and of itself, represents a process that is generally *unsane.* There's lots of reasons for that, and I have written about them elsewhere (*The Secrets of Magic*). It's *unsane* mostly because it reduces our experiences, limits our choices and options, and by labeling us, puts us in a box. It's unsane because it leads to a poor adjustment to eating and exercising reality.

Actually, we *are* so much more than what we think, feel, say, or do. We *are* more than our skills, our experiences, our history, our ideas, our associations, our jobs, our careers, our financial status, etc. We are so much more than our body and our habits. To limit ourselves and define ourselves exclusively by any one of these or a hundred other things prevents us from truly recognizing and owning our ever-changing, always transcending self.

Suppose you learned to play the *"I'm so much more than anything I experience..."* Game? By dis-identifying, we learn to step out of narrow and rigid roles, definitions, labels, etc. and discover a larger sense of ourselves, which, makes for a greater sense of self-dignity and worth.

Now say *"No!"* to the idea— the stupidity of thinking that you *are* your weight, shape, body, activities, emotions, etc. Declare that you *are* so much more than any of that. Then say a thunderous *"Yes!"* to the idea that you will not sell your self to your looks. "I am so much more than my body."

To play this Game, you have to separate *person* and *behavior* in your mind so that it can then affect your talk and your emotions. Take these ideas, if you want to play this Game, and use them as the form and structure of the way you frame things. Then invent some rules about the actions and interactions that express and support this way of framing things.

Decide to play it year round, night and day. Decide to let it become your default frame of reference. Then constantly check the play as the referee of your own mind, blowing the whistle on any behavior, verbalization, tone, expression that doesn't support yourself as so much more than your expressions. Now, let that Game begin!

"I am more than my body, my mind, my emotions, experiences, etc. These are but expressions of me, but not *me.*"

"I have No Control Over My Eating" Game
If you talk this way to yourself, if you have mapped this out as your frame about yourself, then you know all too well what a *dragon state*

this Game can create. To imagine and frame ourselves as powerless, having no control, being out-of-control, etc., recruits us to play the Victim Game. People usually learn to play this Game after they have failed at dieting. They conclude erroneously that they have no "will power." Then, instead of learning how to take effective action, we waste our mental and emotional powers on whining, complaining, feeling worthless, etc.

Doing that further invites us to play Games of self-deception as it prevents us from truly recognizing our basic powers and owning those powers. This reveals some of the devilishness of the Frame Game—by abdicating our most basic powers, we play the Game of helplessness, "I have no choice." "I can't help myself.' "I'm powerless over this." And such games inevitably lead to the Binging Frame Game, the Compulsive Eating Frame Game, etc.

To slay the dragon that this Frame Game generates, we will want to play two Games:

    1) "It's My Power Zone Frame Game and I can Control my Brain if I want to."

    2) *"My Choices are Mine!* And nothing, but nothing can take away that ultimate Freedom!"

The Choice Frame Game
A Game for Slaying, Taming, and/or Transforming Dragons

Here's a Game to play that will drive the dragon out into the open and give you a chance to slay it. Pick up your fork at your next meal and say aloud, "I choose to eat this." Continue to do so with every bite. When you get to the place that you are over-eating, turn your *actions* into *expressed choices.* Say aloud,

    "I choose to over-eat as I stuff this also into my mouth. It's my personal choice to over-eat, to become fatter, and to wear this on my thighs!"

After a hundred or two times of saying that, then shift to some other expressions that also allow you to claim total ownership of your actions.

    "I am a complete victim to what my hand is doing every time it picks up more food and stuffs it into my mouth. I accept no responsibility for *how* or *what* I am eating. My genes are making me do this. My parents are forcing me even this very moment to continue this insanity.'

When you are with friends and associates, and the subject of eating, exercising, health, fitness, energy, weight, etc. comes up, stand up and announce to them all:

"I have chosen to look like this. It's been my choice, not always conscious, in fact, often I haven't been mindful enough to even think about what I've been doing to my body, but it's all been because at some level, I have chosen to do it. Today it no longer really matters why I made those choices, it only matters that I have now chosen a different path."

These lines will flush out the dragons. Count on it. When you do this, the Dragons will actually come out blaming, accusing, denying, defending, insulting, etc. Just let them. And as they do, just notice them. And as you recognize that they are just old mind frames that have caused, contributed, and/or supported you current situation, just enjoy spotting the dragons. Let a smirk come over your face as you look and listen to these old dragons, knowing that they shall soon be slain or tamed.

By the way, dragon frames hate being laughed at. The sword of humor, especially self-respectful humor that mocks at an old thought or feeling as just a thought or feeling absolutely terrifies a dragon state. Let it. It's your power.

Another Dragon Slaying Game
The *Unnoticed Personal Power* Frame Game

Here's a Game that I've often play with people who want to lose weight. Again, it helps to increase one's conscious awareness of actual choices available. It helps to tame the dragons as it simultaneously flushes them out.

"Tom, you say that your ideal body weight would be 165 pounds, but that you're now at 210 and that you've been as high as 230. The question I have for you is this. Why don't you weigh 350 or 480?"

"Are you crazy? I could never stand myself weighing 350 pounds. That would be disgusting!"

"Ah, so you do have a disgust level! That's great to know. It must also mean that you do have a lot of personal power to stop yourself from preventing yourself from getting *that* fat. You must have self-control powers that you haven't noticed until now. Sounds like you're pretty skilled at *not* getting up to 350 pounds."

"Yeah, I guess I am."

"How do you do that?"

"I just refuse to go there. .."

"Ah, the Stubbornness strategy! Good. That means you could play the 'I stubbornly refuse to tolerate my body from becoming over-weight.'"

"I wonder what it will be like if you lower your Disgust Level, and stubbornly refuse to go over 180 pounds... I wonder what that would mean for you?"

Excuse Making Frame Games
"Yes, I'd like to lose weight, butt ..."

You know about the *"Yes, but..."* Games. We all play them. And we all have them played on us. We offer a great idea and we hear, "Yes, but that won't work because..." Let me now introduce to you the *"Yes, butt..."* Games. The "Yes, butt..." Games make for larger and larger butts. So, every time you hear yourself using them, just feel your butt growing larger, expanding, ripping the seams of your clothes.

Excuses, excuses, excuses. When it comes to eating and exercising, we all seem to have become highly skilled in excusing ourselves from the fitness, energy level, and slimness that we say we want.

"I'll Start Tomorrow..." Game

"It's All My Genes..." Game

We make excuses by discounting the investment of time, effort, energy, thought, etc. We do so by playing various mental Games.

"What's the Use?" Game

"It Won't Matter That Much" Game

Excuse Refusal Frame Game
As a Dragon Slaying Game

Todd told me that he had more excuses for staying fat than I could shake a stick at.

"You want me to shake a stick at your excuses?" I asked incredulously.

(Laughing) "No, that's just an expression."

"If I shook a stick at your excuses, would that get them to back off and leave you alone?"

"No."

"Then what would? What would get you to stop listening to the voices of all these slithering excuses that worm their way into your mind and poison your ability to take effective action?"

"Okay, enough of that metaphor. I get the point!"

"And...?"

"Well, I suppose I just need to decide that I'm not going to give any validity to the excuses. That they are just stupid excuses and I don't need to listen to them."

"That's all you would have to do? That would do it?"

"Well, I'd have to then take responsibility to act on what I know about eating and exercising."

"And are you willing to do that?"

"Well... "

"And the excuses snake into your mind, wrapping around your cortex and squeezing it until you become their slave...."

"Okay, okay. Yes I'm willing to do that.'

"And now for the final question. Will you do that?"

The Excuse Blow-Out Game

We all create excuses. As children, most of us became pretty skilled at inventing excuses for getting out of things. Something would break, or an accident would occur, and some adult would ask about its cause and we would explain why we should not be held accountable:

"She made me do it."

"He looked at me in a funny way."

"I was tired.

"It just slipped out of my hands."

Thus began our career in excuse making. As we later learned more sophisticated ways of thinking, reasoning, arguing, etc., we became even better at the art of excusing ourselves from responsibility. We even learned we could excuse ourselves by excusing ourselves.

"I'm sorry; excuse me. I'm such a clutz. I never do anything right."

Surprisingly, that often not only gets us off the hook, but brings others to our rescue.

What precisely is an excuse?

Originating from Latin, *ex-* and *causa* (cause or explanation), an excuse is a *an explanation about the cause of something*. And why would we want to "explain" a cause? Typically, to "explain away" our part. In this way, we invent excuses in an attempt to remove blame from something, as an appeal for a pardon, and/or as an exemption or release from something. When we "make an excuse" we offer a way of thinking, reasoning, and arguing to relieve ourselves of responsibility. When we do this, we create a set of ideas so that our "ability" to "respond" does not play front and center to the experience. This makes *an excuse* a set of ideas, beliefs, and understandings about various factors, causes, and contributing influences that brought something about and that leave us feeling unable to act.

Linguistically, an *excuse* is like a noun, a noun that designates a Thing. But have you ever smelled an excuse? Held an excuse in your hands? This noun-like term ("excuse") actually designates a set of actions. This turns it into a pseudo-entity with no external reality. It only exists *in our head* as a way of thinking and punctuating our understandings about "causation." *Excuses* do not exist "out there," they only exist inside.

> This means that an *excuse* involves *a higher (or meta) frame of reference* by which we box up some action or experience. We put the experience into mental boxes by our excuses.

We can now categorize excuses in various ways.

> *Legitimate* excuses— true causes or influences, and illegitimate excuses— reasons that hold no water, explanations that don't make any sense.

> *Accurate* reasons enable us to understand how and why we cannot legitimately blame or accuse ourselves or another.

> *Inaccurate and illegitimate* excuses try to cover up true

responsibility to escape consequences.

Stupid and silly and wimpy excuses that deserve no attention and only sabotage our ongoing development and effectiveness.

Reasoning To Excuse Ourselves from Life

Good "excuses" are those healthy and legitimate reasons that allow us to consider various constraints in reality: physiological constraints, social constraints, time constraints, relationship constraints, health constraints, etc. We should listen to these and intelligently work with them. I typically excuse myself from working 24 hours in a row. There would have to be some kind of emergency situation before I would override basic health constraints. I excuse myself from chasing an idiot driver down the highway because I'm not authorized to do that, don't have the time, don't have the resources to do anything about it if I caught the driver, etc.

There are a lot of *good* excuses. These comprise valid explanations that we use as we conceptualize our world and our role in it.

There are also lots of *bad* excuses... silly, wimpy, and stupid "reasons" that we use to dis-empower ourselves, undermine our effectiveness, let ourselves off the hook from assuming responsibility for ourselves, etc. These are the kinds of excuses that we need to address.

So, what's your "reason" for *not* doing something that you really want to do?

Are you using a frame of *true* explanation or a *mere excuse* that just gets you off the hook so that you don't have to look at what you thought, felt, said or did and take corrective action?

Are you just excusing yourself from work, energy, emotional investment, etc.?

Are you just reverting to a more infantile style of coping?

Some wimpy excuses arise as just old habits, reactive responses with little thought to it. "I would begin to work my plans, but it's just not the right time ... but I'm just too tired to exercise... but I might get embarrassed...

When we find some actual *excuses*, then we have a sick and ill-formed reason that we're using to prevent ourselves from having to face consequences. And that only prevents us from using pain to alter our way of acting.

Do you have any of these false reasons, these excuses that you are sick and tired of? That does not serve you well? That may be stopping you from achieving some of your hopes and dreams? Then bring it on and let's blow it out.

Food Excuses —

- "I won't lose any weight anyway."
- "I'm just going to fail anyway."
- "I'll start tomorrow..."
- "This one time won't count..."
- "Everyone else is eating this."
- "Look at that fat person, I'm not *that* heavy!"
- "It's just in my genes. I'm helpless."
- I put off eating breakfast or the first meal of the day because I know that once I get started, I wont' stop eating. It's like letting a beast out of a cage.
- "I will start afresh tomorrow and do much better."

The Higher Levels of an "Excuse"

So would *you* like to have the ability to eliminate excuses in your life about over-eating, failing to exercise, failure to apply what you know about healthy living? What if you could eliminate all of your excuses from taking effective action about mastering your weight?

Understanding the structure of an "excuse" (how we excuse ourselves from things) and how to utilize our knowledge of that structure enables us to eliminate it.

An excuse involves a multi-level structure so that at the primary level we have *a desire* to achieve or do something (i.e., eat right, exercise, etc.), but at a meta-level we have *"reasons"* that we use that prevent and prohibit us. We use our *justifications* to excuse ourselves. We use disbeliefs to prevent ourselves. We use prohibitions to forbid ourselves. We use skepticism to bathe the desire with doubt. We use ideas that enable us to discount the desire.

This leaves us with patterns whereby we both *want* to do something and *cannot get* ourselves to take action. Do you know that one? The result? We develop maladaptive patterns that fill us with negativism, reluctance, and avoidance.

Diagram:

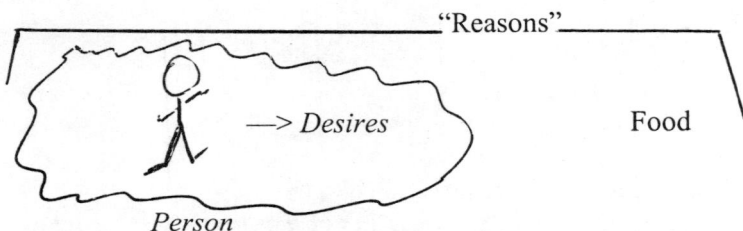

How to Play the Excuse Blow-Out Game
1) Access an Excuse

- Think of something you want to do that's very important to you, an outcome that you know is well-formed and ecological for you, something that would really improve the quality of your life and yet ... just as soon as you do, you find that numerous excuses come to mind which stops you from acting on your desired outcome.

- What would you like to do about X (work, career, health, fitness, relationships, etc.)? Take a moment to imagine just going ahead and doing that thing... and then notice what happens. How do you excuse yourself from it? Listen to your internal voice.

The first step here involves accessing a state wherein you feel an excuse. Now feel that excuse. Notice where you feel it in your body. What does it feel like. In your body? How do you know to call it an excuse?

     Remember, we are going after silly, wimpy, stupid and unuseful excuses with this pattern, not legitimate reasons.

2) Quality Control the Excuse
- Is it just an excuse?
- Do you want this excuse?
- Do you need it?
- Does it serve your life at all? Does it enhance you or empower you?
- If there is some part or facet of the excuse that you might need or want to preserve, what is it? What facets of the excuse may serve a positive purpose for you?

3) Preserve the Values of the Excuse
- Take a moment as you go inside and preserve any part of the excuse that might prove useful to you in some way at some time. Suck out of the excuse any element (a value, belief, understanding) that could be useful. Suck it all out so that the rest of the excuse remains as an empty shell, devoid of any usefulness at all.
- Notice the value of the reason— an understanding, belief, or state that you want to keep with you.. Note it and store it as something you can have apart from this particular stupid excuse.
- Is it now just an excuse? Just an empty shell of an excuse? [Yes]
- If not, repeat until you just have an empty shell of an excuse left.

4) Reject the Empty Shell of the Old Worn Out Excuse
- Access a strong "NO!" state, a "Hell, No!" state. Amplify that state of "Rejection, Refusal, or Disgust" that comes out as a *"No"* fully until you feel it very strongly. Anchor it spatially in a spot and feel it in your hands and in your feet. Let it radiate throughout your body.
- When you have it accessed very strongly, imagine the empty excuse immediately in front of you and step into that excuse with the NO!" state and Stomp on the excuse with the power of your "hell, No!" Stomp it to the ground.

5) Test

- Now imagine the desired activity that's ecological and notice what happens as you think about moving toward it ... What do you feel? What comes to mind? Do you have any excuse lurking that you might use to excuse yourself from life, love, and commitment?

6) Access Your Executive Decision State

- Will you do this? Will you allow it to become an attractor in your mind so that as you think of this activity, how you will do it will simply become a matter of discovery and of building the resources so that you can .. and will. will you not? Go to the part of your mind that makes decisions and commission it to go ahead and decide to engage in your desired activity.

The "Forgiveness" Frame Game

Who or what do you need to forgive in order to release the fat? An interesting question, isn't it? Judy Wardell (1985) talks about this in her book, *Thin Within.*

"Our overweight bodies are a reflection of our resentments, guilt feelings, and unforgiven feelings. In order to release the excess weight, we must first release those resentments and guilt feelings." (p. 139)

If beliefs and other ideas (as frames of mind) can psychologically affect us so that our neurology responses, then it makes sense that "releasing" angers, resentments, frustrations, disappointments, traumas, etc. can have a powerful effect on "releasing" weight. Could it be that the "weight" that we carry in our heart could invite corresponding "weight" in our body?

For year I saw this repeatedly in my psychotherapy practice. As people became free and lighter in their mind and emotions, they got lighter in their bodies. Give yourself permission to forgive ... forgiveness is for you—to keep your spirit sweet, to release you from hurts, to free you from prisons of hate and malice. Release the idea that what has happened determines your future. Say *"No!"* to that nonsense. What determines your future is your current values and visions.

Other Dragon Slaying Games

There's lots of ways to tame, slay, and transform Dragons. See *Dragon Slaying* (2000) for an entire treatment of that subject. For skill at the best Dragon Slaying sword that you can wield, learn to use the Language Precision questions of the Meta-Model (see *The Secrets of Magic,* 1998). When we ask specificity questions (i.e., when, what, where, how, in what way, etc.), we pull apart the linguistic and semantic threads of the fabric of that conceptual reality. It begins to unglue the construction so that it loses its coherence. This destabilizes the frame as it de-constructs the "logic" and structure of the frames.

The Fear of Being Thin

Many people simply *fear* becoming slim or thin. Well, more accurately, they *fear* the *meanings* they give to being slim" or "thin." As they have constructed various *meanings* about the significance of the *idea* of losing weight and becoming slim, trim, and attractive, they now fear those meanings. Those meanings scare the hell out of them.

What could be so scary about *ideas?*

Well, if becoming thin *means* that one is open to seduction and may become a target of the interest and desire of others, that could induce a fear state in some people. If it *means* that one becomes unprotected and vulnerable to the advances of others, or if it *reminds* one of the feelings and states when one was young and slim and without resources, it could induce unresourceful states.

Being "slim" or "thin" means, is connected to, and signifies sexuality, attractiveness, seductiveness, danger, vulnerability, etc. to lots of people. And with *that* frame of mind, no wonder their self-organizing mind-body cues their neurology to *not* allow them to go there. These kinds of frames need to be de-energized, re-formatted, and reframed. Such persons will probably need to learn to reverse their mind about the old meanings.

"And how, in the name of heaven, does one do that?"

Easy. Use the Reverse Your Mind pattern from NLP. Actually, in NLP this pattern goes under the title of Visual-Kinesthetic Dissociation or "the Phobia Cure." It's all about *reversing your mind* by changing the frames we put around a fear.

The Pattern:

1) Step back from your thoughts as you represent them as a Movie.

Begin by imagining yourself sitting in a movie theater. On the screen in this mental theater, put a black-and white picture of "The Younger You" in the situation *just before* the traumatic events occurred, perhaps you were mocked or teased about your weight.

Freeze-frame that movie as a snap-shot, a scene prior to the movie. Now sit back to watch it with awareness that you have taken a spectator's position to that Younger You. From an outside position notice that you have stepped out of the picture. This will change how you feel *about* it.

As you gain this sense distance, take a moment to full *feel* this feeling of distance as you appreciate this ability to step aside. Because taking this spectator position to your old memories enables you to *begin to learn* from them in new and useful ways.

You might notice that your Younger Self in that memory thought and felt from an unresourceful position than you have now, setting here, and observing that Younger You with your adult mind. And this can give you a new and different perspective, does it not? Now.

2) Step Back to notice the Cinematic Qualities of the Movie.

Since you have stepped back and taken this new position to your thoughts about that Younger Self who experienced some traumatic event, you can now look at the ways you internally represent that memory and keep it alive in your mind today. As you do, just notice as a dispassionate observer the distinctions of sights, sounds, sensations that you use to encode the memory.

As a spectator to your movie, notice how you have encoded the movie and the qualities of it. Notice the cinematic features in terms of the audio and video factors that govern the movie.

Begin with the visual system and just notice whether you have your movie in color or black-and-white? Notice its distance: how close or far? Notice its intensity: how bright or dim? Shift back and forth to notice the effect of the coding. Notice what happens to your sense of comfort or distress when you dim the picture of this unpleasant memory. Suppose you turn down the brightness and do so until it no longer bothers you. How far into the distance do you need to send the picture until you can observe it comfortably?

As you play with these distinctions, you can begin to choose the coding that enable you to *think comfortably about* that memory so that you can stay resourceful and thoughtful in a relaxed and comfortable way.

Consider the sound track of this memory. Do you even have a sound track? What sounds do you hear coming from that movie? What are the quality of tones that you hear? At what volume, pitch, and melody?

Next, check out your language system. What words do you hear from that Younger You? From where do you hear these words coming? Notice their tone, volume, and location.

As you notice how that Younger You feels, what sensations does that person have in his or her body up that on the screen? Where and at what intensity, weight, pressure?

What shifts in these codings enable you to *think comfortably about* that old memory? As you make these alterations in your coding, you can relax in the growing sense of distance and control this gives you.

3) Step back yet a second-time from the Movie.

Now imagine yourself floating out of your body as you sit in the tenth row in the theater and observe all this, and float all the way back to the projection booth. From this point-of-view you can see Today's Self (in the tenth row) watching your Younger You on the screen. As you note the adult you sitting in the theater (seeing the back the head) you can slo see the still picture on the screen.

At this second step-back, if at any time you feel uncomfortable and need to remind yourself that you are watching it and not in the picture, put your hands up on the plexiglass to remind yourself to feel safe and secure in the control booth.

4) From the projection booth, watch the old Movie play out.

Let the initial snapshot play out as a black-and-white movie as you watch the memory from the projection booth. Watch it from the beginning to the end, then let it play beyond the end to a time when the bad scene disappears and see that Younger You in a time and place of safety and pleasure. As you keep watching after the passing of the trauma, move to *a scene of comfort* ... whether it occurred at the same time or whether you have to fast forward your memories to some future event of comfort. When you get to that place, stop the action, and freeze frame the picture.

5) Step in and Rewind.

We will do the next step very quickly using intense speed so that the process will take *one second*. So wait until you receive all of the following instructions regarding how to do it.

In just a moment, you will *rewind this memory movie* in fast rewind mode. As you have seen movies or videos run backwards, you will rewind this movie. Yet you will do it with one significant difference. This time you will do it from **inside** the movie. To do that you will have to *step back into* the movie. Then from that vantage point, you will see a confusion of sights and a jumbling of sounds as everything zooms back to the beginning.

When you experience the fast rewinding, all the people and their actions go backwards. They walk and talk backwards. You walk and talk in reverse. Everything happens in reverse, like rewinding a movie.

Ready? Then, step into that Younger You in *the comfort scene* at the end of the movie, and take a moment to feel those feelings of comfort, safety, and delight fully and completely. Do you feel that comfort scene?

Good. Now push the rewind button and experience it rewinding ... *zoooooooommmmm*. All the way back to the beginning. It only takes a second or two to do that fast rewind, and how did that feel... rewinding from inside the movie?

6) Rewind five times.

Having arrived back to the beginning snapshot, clear the screen in your mind. Take a break so that you can shift your awareness completely. Open your eyes and look around.

Now, starting with the scene of comfort at the end again, *as soon as you see it*, step into it, feel it fully ... and rewind the movie even faster.

As you do this over and over your brain will become more and more proficient and the rewind will go faster and faster until the rewind takes only a second each time. *Zoommmm!*

7) Test the results.

Take a break from this exercise. Now recall the original memory and try as hard as you can to get the original "bad" feelings back. Try really hard. If you cannot, you have succeeded in neutralizing the old pain which frees you from letting that pain serve as a reference (or a frame of reference) in your mind-body system.

Taming Dragons with Love and Acceptance

There's yet another *Taming Dragons Game* that they really hate. It's paradoxical so I will more fully describe it in the next chapter. But in a word, it involves *loving* your dragon.

Consider what happens when you bring the thoughts and feelings of love, compassion, acceptance, and appreciation to something. Imagine *embracing* your dragon. Doing so does not condone or validate as much as it creates a willingness to look an old dragon in the face and to discover its positive values.

How do we do this?

Ah, one of the subjects within the next chapter.

Summary

- When you find a Frame Game that's toxic, that poisons your attitude, your energy, your commitment, you have a dragon. No need to run. Not now, not when you know what to do with it.
- Thought viruses that would undermine our success and effectiveness can be slain or tamed by learning to play various Dragon Slaying/ Taming Frame Games. Now you know some of them. You can find out about many more of them by checking out *Dragon Slaying: Dragons to Princes* (2000).
- Take a stand against the old Frames that would imprison, defeat, control, and sabotage you. Say a

definitive *"Hell, No!"* to such Games.

Now That You Know—Here's What To Do

- What Dragon Games have you played with Food or Exercise? Name them.
- List all of the excuses that you have used and continue to use that stops you from having the health, fitness , and slimness that you want.
- Play *Excuse Blow Out Game* every day this week, blowing out the excuses that stop you. If you have a partner or some associate who would like to blow out their excuses, play this Game with that person.

BE A DRAGON MASTER

AT THE EDGE OF OUR MAPS, WE TEND TO BELIEVE THAT "BEYOND THERE BE DRAGONS..." NOW, AS A DRAGON MASTER, YOU CAN TAME THEM, TRANSFORM THEM, OR SLAY THEM ... AS APPROPRIATE.

**WHICH SHALL IT BE?
WHICH WOULD SERVE YOU BEST?
WHICH DRAGON WILL YOU TAKE CARE OF FIRST?
HOW CONFIDENT WILL YOU FEEL ABOUT TAKING CHARGE OF YOUR LIFE WHEN YOU HAVE MASTERED ANY AND ALL SUCH DRAGONS?**

Chapter 10

WHEN THE OLD GAMES NO LONGER MAKE SENSE

"Would you like to play some Games
that simply preclude you from playing the old Games?"
"I'd have to give them up?"
"Not exactly, it's more like just not finding them
useful or valuable anymore
and then they would simply vanish away."

Games in This Chapter
The Acceptance Game
The Personal Dignity Game
"It's just Food" Game
"Food for Hunger" Game
The Eating Awareness Game
The Solution Orientation Game
Eating as "Flow" Game

- *Suppose* there were some *frames of mind* ... frames that once you adopted as your way of thinking and perceiving would totally eliminate the old Games.
- *Suppose* that these very frames of mind would simply prevent and preclude the old Frame Games from ever being activated?
- *Suppose* that we could find or design some higher

mental frames which we could use to innoculate us against some of the toxic Frame Games that we've played?

Would you be interested?

The Games that I've collected and described in this chapter are precisely of this nature. When you "set your mind" in the frameworks of these frames, the ways of thinking, feeling, perceiving, and acting of the old Games no longer make any sense. To the extent that you learn to play *these* Frame Games, you *cannot* play the old Games. They innoculate you against them. They preclude you from going there.

Actually, we have already covered a few of these Frame Games. You experienced three such Frame Games in chapter 3 when we introduced the *Power Zone Frame Game* and the Frame Games of uttering a powerful *"No!"* and *"Yes!"* As you play those Games, they simply preclude you from blaming, excusing, whining, playing helpless, wishing your life away, etc.

Then there was the *Empowerment Frame Game* in Chapter 4 that coached you into playing the Game of fully owning your personal powers so that you could "power up" and take effective action. Remember that one? When you play that one, it precludes many of the old Frame Games that have not served you well at all.

How well do you play the *"I Can Say 'No!' and Mean it!"* Game? By learning the art of saying *"No!"* with power and dignity, we can then really say a definitive *"Yes!"* to the things that we truly want. Doing this simply precludes so many of the old Frame Games. The power to say "No!", gives us the power to set limits. If we can't say "No!" we can't really say "Yes!" So, just for skill development, practice saying "No" for no good reason. Think of it as just part of learning to be powerful as you move through the world.

The *Acceptance / Appreciation* Frame Game

The *Acceptance* Game is one not often played by many people. Accepting *what is* would not have allowed most western cultures to have progressed as rapidly or as extensively as we have. Non-acceptance of disease, ignorance, crime, superstition, etc. have allowed us to push back the curtains of knowledge and pushed into new domains. Obviously, there is a place and time for non-acceptance, for intolerance. There's also a time and place for *acceptance.* Perhaps it's the western orientation toward non-acceptance, for changing things, for being unsatisfied with the current conditions, etc. that have caused so many of the stress diseases to become so prevalent.

In terms of food, eating, our bodies, exercise, etc., we also seem very non-accepting and often this non-acceptance shows up in the *Judgment Games.* By way of contrast to judging ourselves, our bodies, our weight, our shape, etc. is the Game of *Acceptance.* We accept that our bodies are fallible, imperfect, that it has flaws, etc. We also accept that eating more than we need will cause us to gain weight and to get fat. We accept the fact that our bodies were made for activity; that we need exercise. That this is not a bad thing, but the way our bodies work.

How do you play this Game?

Think of something small and simple that you *accept* yet may not like. Acceptance differs from appreciation in precisely that—we open our arms wide and warmly in *appreciation* because what we *want* to warmly welcome it. We find it so pleasant. By way of contrast, with *acceptance* we welcome in what we may not like or what we may not experience as pleasant at all. But we accept it.

For example, I accept the fact that it's raining even though I might prefer things if the sun were shining. I accept that there's going to be bumper-to-bumper traffic in the city at rush hour. It's not my preference. It's not my highest desire. But it "is." So, instead of getting myself all worked up about it, I "accept" it. I accept that babies mess their diapers, that cat boxes have to be changed, that we have to dust, that we have to put more gasoline in the car.

Acceptance—the easy and gentle welcoming in of unpleasant realities, not because of desire, but because of the ego strength to recognize the world for what it "is." Pick something small and simple that you accept without really liking and just notice the state of mind and body you experience when you fully re-experience that thing.

Now, use this reference as your *frame* so that you can play an entirely new Game. As you are thinking and feeling and being *this way* in the experience of simply accepting what is, and feeling that gentle acceptance fully and completely in a way that you find resourceful, apply all of this expression of the frame of acceptance to eating, to food, to your body's weight, shape, size, etc., to the process of learning a new diet, a new way of eating, a new way of exercising, etc.

As you begin to play the "I accept myself, my body and the processes involved in health, fitness, and being slim," just notice how you will play this Game, when, where, with whom, why... especially the why. And just accept the fact that this is a marvelous Game to play. In fact, begin now to *appreciate* your ability to play this new Game.

As you did with acceptance, do with **appreciation.** Think of something small and simple that you can so easily appreciate: holding a new born baby, watching a bunch of kittens play, or a glorious sunrise, or enjoying a good book with a cup of coffee. Pick whatever does it for you. And again, just experience the feelings and thoughts that come along with that state of simple and pure *appreciation*.

This differs from acceptance. Now you *warmly welcome* the referent into your presence. Notice the differences in how you breathe, look, move, your posture, etc. And again, use this as your *reference* for the *frame of appreciation* and apply it to eating, food, yourself, your body weight, size, and shape, and to the process of living in a healthier and more slim way.

Accepting and appreciating our bodies enables us to understand how they work best. This enables us to begin to trust the mechanism or experience of "hunger" as a friend, a valuable signal. Then, by using true hunger as an organism message, we will be able to play the *Eating for Hunger Game*, which, in turn, enables us to stop all of the Psycho-Eating.

In this new Game, we learn to ask new questions

Do I feel better?

Do I feel slimmer, thinner?

Are my clothes fitter better?

Do I have more energy and vitality?

Rising Up to Play the "Awesome" Frame Game
Or, The "Personal Dignity" Frame Game

Why stop with just *appreciation*? I like going on to get a reference of *awe* and then playing a Game that so few people play, the Game of recognizing yourself as an Awesome person—full of human worth and value; an awesome miracle, a person to be celebrated. Talk about Game that will eliminate and prevent the old judgment and self-contempt Games, this one will do it!

Imagine it. Just suppose you woke up in the morning and you not only have a frame of mind that when you eat and exercise you do so from a state of *acceptance and appreciation,* but that you actually look upon yourself with so much personal dignity, that you couldn't mistreat your body or health by mis-eating or abusing food. Take a moment and imagine that Game... Go ahead.

Wouldn't that be a trip? Well, what's stopping you from playing that one? Ah, you need some fabulous concepts and ideas that will allow you to play it. Okay. Here they come.

The idea of how we appraise or "esteem" our value, important, and significance as human beings is described in psychological and philosophical literature as "self-esteem." And typically, most people in most cultures start from the assumption (and it's a toxic one), that our value is conditional. Yet when we start there, then we have to "earn" or "prove" our worthwhileness. Talk about a sick frame of reference. Do you think about newborn babies like that?

> "Yeah, that baby is worthless! Can't do a thing. Can't pull it's own weight around here. I don't know why we put up with it."

Of course not.

Actually we confuse categories. We take the category of self-confidence and falsely assume that *self-confidence* is the same as *self-esteem.* Wrong. These are two very, very different concepts.

Confidence refers to the faith that I have in my skills and abilities, the confidence I put in my ability to *do* something. And everybody has some confidences. Everybody also has lots of things wherein they have no confidence.

Esteem refers to our appraisal of worth and value as a human being, in who we are *existentially* as members of the human race. It has nothing to do with what we can *do,* it has to do with what we *are.*

To confuse the two confuses human *beings* with human *doings.* Now, knowing that you can easily play the Game of "My Human Worth and Value is a Given!" You can play, "Nobody gave it to me, nobody can take my Esteem away from me!" You can play the Game, "I'm un-rate-able; my worth and value is unconditional and unlimited!"

To get the feeling, think of something that you consider just absolutely *awesome*: the infinite universe of stars and planets and solar systems, the wonder and magic of a newborn baby, the mystery of life, a glorious sunset, or whatever for you elicits the sense of awe, even worship. Get that reference and let it totally touch your mind and heart. Feel it fully. And now, using that reference as your *frame* for the new Frame Game of personal dignity, feel all of that about *yourself!* Set that as your frame about your body, about eating, about exercising. And as you experience the sense of personal dignity (or self-esteem) imagine eating and exercising in the days and months and years to come from that frame of mind.

"It's Just Food" Game

If food is just that— food, just fuel for our metabolism, then as we learn to operate from this frame and play this Game, food will become less and less important to us and will play and increasingly less powerful role in our psyche. This happened to me. And it wasn't that I planned it; it just happened as I learned about my own neuro-semantics of food. As I discovered *the meanings* that I had come to attribute to and link up with "food," and realize that I didn't need to give it *that much meaning,* I simply stopped.

So did Rush Limbaugh. If you saw Rush in the early 1990s on television (whether on his TV show or on some interview) you saw a very large man. When I tuned into CNBC on January first, 2000 and saw Tim Russert interviewing Rush, what kept my attention for some time was how slim he looked. I had never seen him looking like that. Russ had lost 110 pounds between 1997 and 1999.

Apparently it was the first time Rush had talked about it. It seems that he had lost 110 pounds and had kept it off for some time.

How did he do it?

Well, for one thing he "totally changed" his eating lifestyle. He had cut out all fast foods, salty snack foods, most wines and red meats, and besides that, he didn't exercise. He didn't like the Atkinson diet at all and spoke strongly against it (as only Rush can!). He weighs daily because "the scale doesn't lie" whereas the feel of the clothes isn't all that accurate.

But more than those specific behavior changes, he changed his frame. And so he played a very different Game with food.

> "Once I was always thinking about food. I thought about what I was going to eat all day long. Food and eating was always on my mind. In fact, I couldn't get it off of my mind. Now it seems like an interference."
>
> "An interference?" Tim asked.
>
> "Yea, a bother. Oh, sure I still go out for two-hour luncheons, but it's just part of business. Food just not all that important to me."

Now there's a different frame of mind. That's a different attitude, a different Game.

"Eating Only For Hunger" Frame Game

Here's a Game. Suppose you decided to eat *only* when you truly feel hungry? Imagine that. What if you committed yourself to eat *only* for hunger? Would that change things? How would it?

To eat only for hunger, of course, we have to learn how to notice and gauge our hunger feelings, and that means re-acquainting ourselves with our bodies.

- How hungry am I on a scale from 1 to 10?
- Could I feel more hungry? Less hungry?
- What if I just committed myself to not eat until I felt hungry on my hunger scale at a level of 5 or 6?
- What if I simply refuse to eat when my hunger is under 4?
- What changes or alterations in my life style would this commitment call for?

Since our bodies need food to provide us energy, *hunger* operates as the body's natural signal that we need more fuel. It gives us a cue to now eat. So, the rule that governs this Frame Game is simply: eat only when you truly feel hungry.

Doesn't that seem simple?

Don't be fooled, *it is not.*

And why not?

Because, in order to comply with this rule, we have to learn to discern the feeling of physical hunger from psychological hungers and emotions (i.e., anxiety, depression, moodiness, loneliness, anger, etc.). If we eat only when we're hungry, then we eat for one primary purpose, to satisfy the hunger. This means that we have to rediscover the "pangs of hunger" so that we respond to that signal instead of other feelings of discomfort.

Try it on.

> "I will eat only for hunger, for the fuel that increases my energy and vitality."

And conversely,

> "I will not eat because its 'time' to eat, or because I feel upset, angry, needing to fit in socially, to merely please others, etc."

How does this new program settle in your mind? What comes to mind when you utter these statements in the interior of yourself?

The process of learning to eat only for hunger and for fuel means learning to listen to our body anew. The fact is, unfortunately, that most of us typically eat for reasons other than hunger.

To assist in this we can use a *Hunger* Scale in order to gauge precisely how hungry we are when we eat and after we eat. If hunger is actually the only legitimate reason for eating, then we need to make sure that we truly feel hungry when we eat. Refuse to eat for any other reason. Use the hunger scale as a habit breaker.

If we are not hungry, then what are we?

Bored	Looking for a distraction
Tired	Frustrated
Tense	Anxious
Thirsty	Watching the clock
Angry	Lonely
Depressed	Wanting comfort or reassurance
Wanting to chew or suck	
Experiencing indigestion	

By learning to take a moment to think before we eat, we can cue ourselves that calories ought to be tasted, not wasted.

What are your eating triggers:

Parties	Restaurants
Buffets	Weddings
Diets	Eating alone
Birthdays	Congratulating yourself
Loneliness	Feeling fat
Stress	Cooking
Boredom	Tiredness
Frustration	Fear
Time to eat	Insomnia
Depressed	Angry

What activities do you have with which to displace eating? To stop misusing food and to eat only for hunger, we will need some other choices, when we would otherwise defer to eating. It can be as simple as going for a walk or engaging in any kind of activity, to taking a few moments to breathe deeply and enjoy some little wonder (a child, a cat or dog, art work, etc.) to increase the beauty, pleasure, and mystery in your life. Engaging a specific sense (listening to music, straightening out a room, washing fresh fruit, etc.) can also keep us engaged and refocus our attention.

As you practice playing this Game, recognize that because your stomach has sensory nerves, you only need to accept and embrace the sense of hunger in order to receive those signals. This means *noticing*, quieting yourself to notice, differentiating between psychological hungers (i.e., upset, anxiety, nervousness, emptiness, etc.) and physiological hunger.

What does "hunger" feel like to you?

Don't know? Then stop eating for awhile. You'll find out. Get out for a 30 minutes of walking. Typically, we experience hunger as empty feelings in the stomach, rumblings, loss of energy, light-headedness, etc.

Eating Awareness Frame Game

We can play *the Awareness Game* in two ways. One way occurs when we decide to become aware of the sensory qualities of food: smells and tastes, what it looks like, how it feels in our mouth and stomach, what it looks like, etc. This brings us back to sensory awareness. At this level, we notice the temperature of the food, texture, etc. And it raises some interesting questions.

- At what level of awareness do I eat?
- Do I eat at the primary level?
- How often do I eat from a meta-level where I eat for various emotional needs?

We'll describe this Game more fully in the next chapter when we play the *Sensory Delight* Game.

Another kind of Food Awareness Game that we can play has to do with becoming *mindful* of our Eating Habits. To more effectively play this eating awareness Game, it helps to begin to chart eating experiences. To play this Game, simply record the following about your food intake:

Time: (When)
Place: (Where)
Food: (What)
Reason: (Why?)
Hunger Level (0 - 10 prior to eating, and when finished)

Pete Cohen and Judith Verity in their *NLP Lighten Up* programs (1998, 1999) write,

"The key to changing your eating habits is awareness. Look for the times that you eat during the day.

How much are you eating?

Do you enjoy every bite?

What are your food choices?" (1998, p. 36)

Corsetty and Pearson in *Healthy Habits* really believe in recording and so have devoted an entire chapter to this developing awareness of food and nutritional habits. They write:

"Studies have shown that the most effective tool for taking off unwanted ponds and keeping them off involves keeping track of the food intake. Recording the amount and type of food you eat makes you more aware of unnecessary eating." (p. 15)

Journaling and charting how we play the Eating Game enables us to find the roadblocks in our way as well as the problematic factors: the problem environments, times, and emotions. Naming the Game that we're playing with food brings greater awareness and that increases choice and control.

Corsetty and Pearson suggest a Food Journal based upon this format:

Date: _____

What Foods I Ate	— Amount —	Time —	Location —	Emotions Felt Before/ After

    This is what Patricia did. Before using *Games Slim People Play* she was eating at least three meals a day plus snacking. Then, just by reading

> "... and without consciously doing too much of anything, I just 'lost' a lot of my appetite and I find myself not eating very much because I'm not all that hungry. When I looked at that, I saw clearly that my previous meals were not prepared and eating because I was truly hungry, but because i was bored, wanted to be distracted and/or because it 'was time to eat.'"

Welcoming Afresh Internal Hunger Cues

    All of this suggests one Game which slim people play that over-weight people and dieters do not play. Slim people play, "I'll trust my body's internal cues." Dieters do not. They trust some formula for caloric intake, some dietary plan, and other external cues.

    Janet Polivy and Peter Herman in *Breaking the Diet Habit* (1983) in extensive research experiments have concluded that to the extent that one's eating is controlled by external factors, it cannot be as responsive to other sorts of cues (e.g., hunger and satiety). They suggest that this leads to the "what you see is what you eat" tendency of the over-weight.

> "All these studies show that for overweight people, their eyes are, if not bigger, at least more influential, than their stomachs. The reason this is true is that the overweight people studied in these experiments are so busy fighting against their natural weights that they no longer pay attention to the dictates of their hunger and satiety feelings." (p. 140)

> "As long as the dieter ignores hunger but exerts rigid control over what food cues are in sight and what is allowed into the

mouth, this unnatural eating may seem to work. Unfortunately, being out of touch with the body's messages of hunger and fullness may leave the dieter susceptible to other influences." (p. 141)

By way of contrast, the naturally slim and those who do not diet regulate their eating according to their stomachs and so eat more appropriately. Dieters eat according to the formula of their diet, whatever that be. But if a dieter "breaks" the diet, or even *thinks* that he or she has broken it, will typically eat *much more* than the non-dieter. Polivy and Herman (1983) wondered about this and so explored the reasons behind it.

"Every dieter that we later spoke to about these results immediately recognized this as what we have come to call the 'what-the-hell effect.' That is, the subjects had not simply been preloaded, as in previous studies using sandwiches; they had been forced to break their diets. Our subjects hadn't even fasted for 5 hours before the experiment. In fact, our subjects participated in this milkshake and ice cream study one or two hours after lunch or dinner. Thus, there was no way the milkshakes could be incorporated into their daily caloric limit. Once their diets were broken by the milkshakes, the dieters threw restraint to the wind and enjoyed their ice cream.

"This study betrays, in a nutshell, the problem of dieting. As long as things go well, as long as there are no disruptions, one can keep the lid on one's food consumption without counting on the normal regulatory influences of hunger and satiety. But just disturb the system—disrupt the fragile mental controls, caloric quotas, and other gimmicks holding the diet together—and there is nothing short of one's physical capacity that can be relied upon as a brake. If satiety signals are not normally used as *the* inhibition of eating, their usefulness may atrophy; if one decides to use charted caloric quotas as one's guide instead, satiety cues may not be available as an emergency back-up." (pp. 142-143)

Ah, another Game. The *"What the Hell!"* Game. Dieters will take the experience of one mistake in sticking to the diet and treat it as a complete failure. Most dieters know this Game: *"I've blown it. Why bother trying now? I might as well enjoy myself. I will start again tomorrow.* " What causes this? These types of thoughts as their frames.

In another study, Polivy and Herman gave their subjects two 8-ounce servings of chocolate pudding as their "pretaste." They told half of them that this pudding was a "rich, gourmet, pudding-type desert." They told the other half that they were eating a "dietetic, low calorie, pudding-type dessert." Actually, half the time the pudding actually was low calorie and half the time it was very high calorie. It was all a matter of chance. Yet whether the actual calories matched the description, the actual caloric value was independent of the reputed caloric value.

> "The actual number of calories in the pudding turned out to have no effect on how much test food any of our subjects subsequently ate, whether they were dieters or not. ...However, what the subject *thought* about the caloric content of the puddings did make a difference. Non-dieters ate slightly more after a pudding they thought was low calorie. Dieters, as we had by now come to expect, ate more after a pudding they thought was *high* calorie. Thus, just thinking that they had broken their diets caused our dieters to overeat, whereas thinking they had only eaten some low calorie, dietetic pudding allowed them to retain their control and eat very little." (p. 144)

These studies show the importance of using our *internal signals of hunger and fullness* rather than relying upon external cues. Such signals are more reliable and allow us to maintain control easier. When trying to control weight by external factors (diets, calorie formulas, etc.), even simply believing that one has over-eaten leads to the breakdown of self-control. Then, the idea that the dieting has been nullified breaks down normal restraint.

All of this led Polivy and Herman to conclude:

> "People try to fight their natural weight no longer eat in response to the signals that their bodies give; instead, they are at the mercy of the world around them."

"Aiming Toward Solution" Frame Game

With Tom, who I mentioned in Chapter Four, I asked,

"So this sounds like a big problem. But I have a question for you. *When* is the problem of over-eating *hardly ever* a problem at all? What are you doing or where are you at, or who are you with when eating right seems to come easy and naturally to you? Has there ever been a time in your life like that?"

"Sure there has."

"Tell me about it."

And so he did. He began describing *exceptions* to the problem of over-eating. And as he did, he essentially began mapping out for himself another way to navigate this situations that activate his compulsion to mindlessly eat. He later told me that he was genuinely surprised by how the exercise (or Game) of describing *Exceptions* opened him up to alternative ways of operating. He said he felt so much more creative and in control of his life.

Playing the "Tell me about an Exception" Game uses a process popularized in Brief Psychotherapy by de Shazar. It enables us to truly focus on *exceptions* and for building up a solutions out of those times when the problem doesn't occur. The "un-storied" facets of our lives are thereby energized and empower to become a story or frame.

The Eat as "Flow" Game

Suppose you set a frame which would turn your eating itself into a Game—a Game wherein you aimed to become more and more disciplined and self-controlled in your eating and in eating for energy. Making the activity of eating more like *a Game* would prevent it from feeling like *a chore*. What if you could transform your eating so that it had more Game-like features to it? To make it a Game, you would need the following:

1) Specific goals about how much, when, and what to eat. So set some goals that you can precisely measure about eating.

2) Direct and immediate feedback. What will you use to give you immediate feedback about your eating?

3) Challenges and skills. Do your skills match the challenges of the Game? If your skills far outmatch the challenges, you'll get bored and quit. If the challenges far outweigh your skills, you'll feel overwhelmed and defeated and so will quit.

4) Demanding focus. Does the Game and its rules set up a

demanding focus for you while you're playing it?

If this list looks or sounds familiar, it might just remind you of the prerequisites for "flow" as described by research psychologist, Mihaly Csikszentmihalyi. Turning any activity into a flow activity involves first bringing conscious awareness to develop skill involving a complex set of interactions for the purpose of becoming highly skilled and disciplined. Then comes lots of focused and concentrated practice. This enables us to habituate the high level skills of excellence so that they just become automatic. When this happens, then like an athlete "in the zone," we can quickly step back into the activity and automatically reclaim the high level skills that enable us to operate like a pro— like an expert.

- How do we turn the idea of lifestyle fitness and healthy eating into a "flow" experience?
- What if eating and exercising were more Game-like so that eating right become more of a flow experience?

"Flow" refers to one of those peak experiences that we all happen upon from time to time when it seems like everything goes away and we become totally caught up in the moment, lost in time and space. Our sense of self, time, environment, etc. just disappears and we find ourselves almost merged into some activity. It can be as simple as gardening, running, meditating, or as complex as mountain climbing, inventing a new gadget, figuring out a mathematical problem, writing a novel, reading a book, etc.

Mihaly Csikszentmihalyi has spent his life researching and studying "flow" experiences. It began by chance from his original studies in "happiness" and creativity. As a result, he has written several books on "Flow" and has made explicit the structure of a "flow" experience. In doing so, he has specified the requirements and conditions under which the "flow" state emerges.

As an overview, "flow" operates within a channel between the experiences of boredom and challenge and these experiences are functions of skill and anxiety (see figure 10:1). Think about two axes, challenge and skills. When our *skills* are really low, it's easy to feel overwhelmed by the *challenges* we face. As our *skills* increase so may we become bored and feel that lack of challenge. When the *challenges* before us are low, again this invites boredom in. Yet as the ***challenges*** increase, we may feel overwhelmed.

The balance of sufficient challenge for our skills and always increasing the challenges to fit the new and ever-changing state of our skills is what allows us to get into the flow channel.

This model informs us about the structure of "flow" as a state, and as a *Frame Game*. If we take any activity and play with it by setting small but ever-increasing goals, so that we adopt the attitude of looking forward to the ever-increasing challenge, one day at a time, and it transforms the activity into a Game.

Figure 10:1

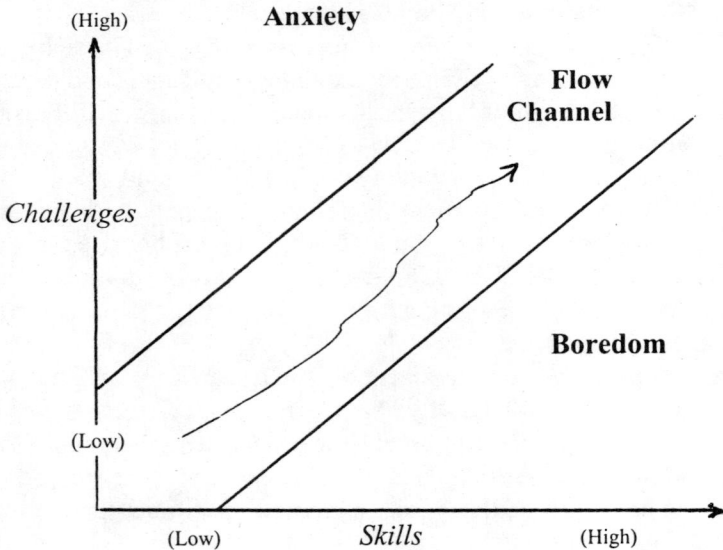

And if we play the Game with an overview of the larger vision and values so that we can see how it all fits together, then we have a sense, on a daily basis, of how it all counts and is important.

As the "Flow" model balances boredom and challenge, it gives us a way to play the "Eating for Hunger" Game, or the "Sensory Delight" Game (or any of the other Healthy Food Frame Games) in a way that everyday life gives us lots of opportunities to have fun in the way we eat and exercise.

This new Game allows our skill enhancement to overcome the challenges that might otherwise overwhelm us or lead to boredom. It enables us to develop a balance so that we don't come up too low on skills and feel overwhelmed or too high skills for the tasks at hand and feel bored. We enter into the flow channel when we have just the right amount of skill and challenge to keep life (i.e., eating and exercising) interesting.

In order to experience an activity as a "flow activity" we have to establish numerous frames so that we no longer have to "think" about ourselves, our successes or failures, etc. Rather our focus becomes totally absorbed in the experience or activity itself so that we lose awareness of self, time, purposes, etc.

To play the Flow Frame Game, make sure that you have the following in place:

1) Goals for your eating, exercising, weight loss. Specific desired outcomes that you find compelling and exciting.

2) Rules about how to make it happen, how fitness and thinness work, food smartness and exercise intelligence.

3) Feedback so that you get constant information so that you can make course changes in appropriate ways.

When that happens, then there will be a growing complexity of the self as we go through the process. The activities will begin to structure the very contents of our consciousness. That is, we will become much more mindful about what we are doing, how we are doing it, and why. There will be a growing skill that we develop in response to the challenges that we face. Eventually, the development in our the skills will make us more playful and masterful in each phase, which will in turn give a sense of inner freedom and power.

The Conditions of Flow   Eating-and-Exercising as Flow

1) Clear goals:

An objective is distinctly defined that gives us immediate feedback which we can know about instantly.

Specific food and activity goals that begin small and increase. Measurable. Specific. Immediate acknowledgment and validation for reinforcement

2) The opportunities for acting decisively are relatively high.

They are matched by our perceived ability to act. Our personal skills are well suited to the challenges.

Skills in food choosing, in eating consciously, in refusing some foods, and in learning to taste anew, skills in seeing opportunities for introducing more activity in everyday life, for pushing self little by little into more activity.

3) Action and awareness merge; one-pointedness of mind.

Intense focus on taste and texture of food when eating, losing our former higher levels of mind about food, and coming to our senses in the experience of eating. Intensely focusing on other pleasurable activities, such as walking, running, swimming, walking stairs, etc.

4) Concentration on the task at hand.

Irrelevant stimuli disappear from consciousness as our worries and concerns are temporarily suspended.

Make the eating and exercising experiences of concentration so that we can get lost in them and thereby enjoy them for what the sensory delights that they do present.

5) A sense of personal control.

Ownership of choice, decision, responsibility for healthy choices and habits.

6) Loss of self-consciousness and a transcendence of ego boundaries.

A sense of growing and of being part of something greater.

Focus on how our body feels while eating, exercising, on experiences of sensory pleasures in eating, breathing, relaxing, etc.

7) Altered sense of time which usually seems to pass faster.

Allow yourself to get lost in the moment of the experience.

8) Experience becomes autotelic.

The activity is worth doing for its own sake.

Recognize the value of eating for fuel to increase your energy and exercising for the expression of that energy.

Summary

- By becoming fully engaged in playing some Games simply doesn't allow us to play other Games. That's the idea we have pursued in this chapter. We seek to learn such powerful and engaging Games that, in playing them, they disallow and preclude the old Frame Games that were disastrous.

- Games are just Games—just a set of actions, interactions, relationships, and ways of thinking, feeling, and talking—that allow us to bring out our best and operate in a much more resourceful way in the world.

- When we are fully engaged in living our lives with energy and vitality, with purpose and meaning, with a sense of our own innate dignity and worthwhileness, the old sick and fat dragons that would invite us out to play don't have a chance.

Now That You Know—Here's What To Do

- Which Game in this chapter would you like to first install as a Healthy Food Game in your life?

- Set aside time every day this week to rehearse that Game and do so until it feels normal, right, and automatic.

PART IV:

FRAME GAMES
FOR SUSTAINABLE

HEALTHY
EATING AND EXERCISING

FRAME GAMES
FOR A NEW MIND
ABOUT FOOD

Frame Games for Healthy Eating

Our bodies require fuel. There's no question about that. So, to supply fuel, we eat. We *must* eat if we want energy, vitality, an active lifestyle, movement, and a healthy metabolism. And that's pretty much it, we don't need to eat for other reasons. All other eating is *Psycho-Eating*.

When we add *psychology* to food (that is, the Frame Games that we play), we create a mix for some real problems, as the obesity statistics and dieting fads indicate. Anything other than this sets a frame about food that will not serve us well.

Designing New Frames of Mind

- What are the healthy and empowering frames that facilitate the right kind of eating so that we never have to diet?

- The kind of eating that gives us energy, vitality, and slimness?

All of these depend, of course, upon having *a big enough why*. If you have developed your reasons for playing healthier and more vital frame Games, then that compelling purpose will give you the power and motivation to stay with these Games. Test yourself. Do you have a "why" that's big enough and exciting enough to get you out of bed every morning in anticipation of the play today?

The "0-to-5, Present Moment, Eating" Frame Game

Judy Wardell (1985) translates our "Eating for Hunger" Frame Game, into the *Scaling Hunger* Game. The Game goes like this. First you gauge your "hunger" on a scale from 0 to 10. 0 stands for "empty," 5 stands for "Comfortable," and 10 stands for "Stuffed."

Hunger Scale:

10 — Stuffed

5 — Comfortable

0 — Empty

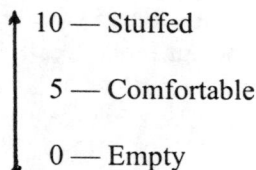

Take a moment to breathe deeply and to notice your stomach. In fact, put your hands on your abdomen and rub it. Notice the sensations that you feel. Are you hungry? Comfortable? Stuffed? Do this every time you walk into the kitchen or dine out and are about to eat. In other words, check in with your body before you eat. "At what level of hunger is your body in at this very moment?"

Of course, lots of people (probably the majority) do not accurately gauge their hunger. They have not been listening to their body. So, as you give yourself permission to eat when you're hungry, re-establish a communicate feedback loop with your body, your stomach.

0-to-5 eating means that you will eat only when you are feeling "empty" and will eat only until you feel "comfortable." This avoids the desperate feelings of "starving" that diets evoke *and* the other extreme of stuffing oneself. It also encourages *present-time* eating, and that, of course, leads to another new Game to play with food: making love to your food so that every bite becomes a sensuous delight. But more about that in a minute.

There's another thing 0-to-5 Hunger Eating does for you. It enables us, over time, to begin to trust our body. At first, most people don't know what "hunger" is. We confuse all kinds of unpleasant, upset, anger, fear, and negative feelings with "hunger." Why? Because *hunger* itself, as a feeling, refers to a generally aversive sensation that's designed to prompt us to eat. At times, wait until your body hits an unequivocal 0. Your body will then let you know that it's time to eat. Eventually you will feel the realigning of your natural rhythms of hunger and comfort.

The Sensory Delight Frame Game

What do you focus on when you eat? Do you focus on the sensory pleasures of the food or the volume of how much you're eating?

Most of us do not see, smell, or taste our food. Really! We gobble. We gulp. We eat without consciousness. We have other things on our minds when we eat. We eat while driving, watching television, arguing, talking, studying, etc.

To play an entirely different Frame Game we will have to "lose our old mind" and "come to our senses." The *Sensory Delight* Frame Game involves setting the frame that you will fully and thoroughly notice, smell, and taste every bite of your food. This will involve a shift in focus so that you concentrate on the taste of the food, discern its texture, temperature, and flavors.

The rules within this Frame Game include the following: Take your time to thoroughly enjoy and delight in every bite that you take. Slow down and notice. This new *Focusing on Food* Game will probably be difficult to hold and so you'll probably want to use some things to keep your mind on the food while you're eating. Write a big sign that gives you a menu list of the qualities of the food to notice: texture, softness, hardness, chewy, moist, dryness, temperature, etc.

As you put yourself into a very intense sensory-aware state, put your fork or spoon down between each and every bite and spend time chewing, tasting, noticing, etc. Aim to reduce your eating speed to about one-fourth your normal speed. And, if you get with a partner to play this Game with you, it will make it even more fun.

"It's Just Food; It Means Nothing Else" Game

As you slow down your eating, use these words to set a new frame for yourself.

"It's just food—fuel for my body and energy for my activities— that's all this is. I refuse to load it up with psychological meaning. It is just nutrition and fuel."

Here too you can repeatedly present to your mind the contrast.

"I once used this food to dull my senses, but now I open all of my senses to notice the food as food. It does not mean love or nurturing, I get those states from relating to people, not food."

In *Meta-States* trainings, we play with a process that we call, *"The Pleasure / Happiness Pattern"* (see Chapter Seven). We use it to identify the meta-levels of meanings that load up a simple activity (whether taking a walk, reading, soaking in a hot bath, playing tennis, etc.). This moves our experience of the primary level pleasure into the realm of meta-level enjoyment. Having used the pattern many times with the activity of eating, it has provided a profound way to understand the higher level *"reasons"* (justifications, rationalizations, memories, concepts, etc.) why we eat and what the experience means to us.

It has also lead us to explore the opposite process, how to *de-pleasure* a simple activity that we have over-loaded with too many meanings. When we have given an activity too much power and influence over us by over-endowing it with too many meanings or too intense and personal meanings—it begins to operate as an addiction. We mentally obsess about it. And we emotionally feel compulsive about it. Yet if it depletes us and makes us less able to cope, then it disorders our lives rather than orders and strengthens us.

How do we *de-pleasure* anything? We set limits on the meanings, "It is just..." We *refuse* to allow it to signify certain things. We set a boundary around the eating experience so that semantically it cannot extend beyond those meaning boundaries . "It's just for fuel and nothing else."

Trusting Your Body Frame Game
"Guided by My Own Body" Game

Research has shown that over-weight people are much more likely to eat in response to *external* cues rather than their own bodies' *internal* hunger signals. They eat by the cue of time, "It's supper time." They eat by the cue of a plate piled before them. Such external cues hook them into the "But I suddenly feel like eating again" Game, whether they are actually hungry or not.

You begin an entirely new Game when you learn to be *guided by your internal hunger*. Those who play this Game operate from the understanding that the body knows... at least your body once knew. Poor eating and exercising habits along with poor mental Frame Games can put us in a place where we feel alienated from our bodies. So, to begin with, let's play the Fritz Perl's Game (Gestalt Therapy) of *Losing our Mind and Coming to Our Senses*.

Most people who over-eat never *truly and fully taste the food.* They gulp. They cram food down their throat. They eat unconsciously. And because they eat unconsciously, they often never notice what they eat or how much they eat.

Spend time with a salad today *just eating and noticing all of the flavors, tastes, textures, smells,* etc. fully and completely. Put your fork down between bites ... and just notice. If there's someone with you, tell that person about it. If you are eating alone, prepare your speech for telling someone about it.

As you "lose your mind" about the hundred thousand other things going on in your life, in your history, in your future, and *come to your senses*, keep cuing your mind to *notice,* and to *pay attention* fully to the food.

Most people find this very, very difficult to do. It will seem unnatural to be fully and completely *present.* But just stay with it.

Write on a three-by-five card, *"Just notice .."*. *"Lose my mind and come to my senses."* Put the card down in front of you.

When you have graduated to being able to more fully enter into the full sensory experience of the food, begin to allow yourself to think and respond like a gourmet to the food. As you do this, you will develop a palate that can enjoy a wide range of foods and make ever more subtle appreciations.

Babies won't eat when they are not hungry. This indicates that we have a natural intelligence in the body about its needs that we need only to rediscover and listen to. To attune ourselves to that native intelligence, we have to develop sensory awareness of it, we need to reacquaint ourselves with it. Sensory pleasure with food necessitates sensory awareness. Learn to eat naked things!

"Tasting things bare is always an experience worth having." (Cohen, p. 167)

Re-educate your taste buds. How do you treat yourself? How much respect to you have for your body?

Food as Fuel Game
Or "It's Not About Food, but Energy" Game

Now that we're no longer eating for the wrong reasons, we're free to eat for the right reasons. Namely, we eat for energy, for fuel, for metabolism, to be alive, etc. So as we recognize and refuse to let eating be about comfort, love, de-stressing, fulfillment, reward, etc., we can say a big bold *"Yes"* to food as being about fuel. "I do not eat to fill a void, to deal with a loss, to comfort myself, etc. I eat to experience the vitality of being alive and to engage fully in the adventure of living."

When we step up to play this Game, suddenly our whole motivation for eating and our intentions about eating change. If *Food is for Energy*, then new questions begin to arise every time I get hungry, namely:

Will this food provide me the kind and quality of energy that I need and want?

What do I want to eat that will make me feel light, energetic, vigorous, and alert?

How will I feel in two hours after eating this?

It's a whole new attitude, a whole new Game. Now eating more sensibly comes more natural and easy. I will not want a lot of fat, greasey foods, fast foods, sugars, etc. Now I will want to be drinking lots of water, eating lots of fruits and vegetables, getting a good balance diet of the food groups, etc.

We know that the kind and quality of the fuel we put into machines makes a lot of difference. The same applies regarding the fuel we put into our bodies. That "fuel" will feed and nourish the complex system of cells that enable us to live, to be healthy, and to do things.

What should you eat?

I cannot improve upon the work of Corsetty and Pearson in their book, *Healthy Habits: Total Conditioning for a Healthy Body and Mind* (2000). In their fifth chapter, they present an excellent "Healthy Habits Formula for Healthy Eating." Quoting from the food exchange method developed and approved by the American Diabetes Association and American Dietetic Association, they offer the following breakdown of food groups that comprise their Healthy Habits Formula:

P = Protein: beef, poultry, fish, pork, shellfish, cheese, rice and beans combined.

M = Milk: yogurt and milk products (slim and low-fat milk are recommended)

S = Starch: cereals, breads, grains, pasta, crackers, etc.

V = Salad-type vegetables: broccoli, celery, lettuce, cucumbers, spinach, etc. Three categories include:

1) Regular: green beans, carrots, peppers, tomatoes, etc.

2) Starchy: corn, peas, lima beans, potatoes.

3) Salad-type: as above.

F = Fruits: there are three different categories for fruits, also.

1) Regular: fruits with high water content: apples, cantaloupes, grapes, peaches, watermelons, etc.

2) Citrus-type: oranges, grapefruits, lemons, tangerines.

3) Starchy: bananas, dates, figs, raisins.

Ft = Fat: Margarine, butter, mayonnaise, oil, salad dressing, nuts.

H^2O = Water: at least 64 ounces (8 glasses) every day.

Food is fuel, pure and simple. From *Healthy Habits* again, Kathy and Judy write:

"In reality, there is only one valid association to make about food: *food is fuel*. Pure and simple. Food is not a reward or a substitute for love. Food is fuel for the body. If you believe otherwise, you have a dysfunctional relationship with food." (p 64)

"If you base your food intake on emotions and cravings rather than on what your body really needs, you may experience an addictive relationship with food." (p. 65)

If this reflects the reality about food, about eating, and about exercising, then listen to how Corsetty and Pearson describe the way they play this Game:

"Because food is fuel, your weight (although determined to some degree by heredity and body size) is directly affected by two factors: intake and utilization of fuel. Intake is what you put into your body ... Utilization is the amount of energy you expend to metabolize calories. You are directly responsible for what you put into your body and how much energy you expend to utilize what you put in." (p. 67)

The "Eating Intelligence" Frame Game

Ultimately, *food* is not our enemy. Not at all. We need food; food is good for us. Food is what provides us fuel for energy and vitality. Pete Cohen (1999) writes,

"Food isn't the enemy. We need the right amount of the right food to make our bodies function at all. It's energy, it's fuel, it's essential." (p.83)

Cohen says that weight management is really *not* about food, but about fuel. Given this, we now need to inquire about the food guidelines that allow us to incorporate better fuel. *What kind of fuel* are you putting into your engine? In the food Game, low octane fuel includes sugars, fats, pre-packaged foods, preservation chemicals, etc. Whereas high octane fuel includes fresh and natural products, unrefined flour and grains, fresh water, fruits and vegetables, etc.

Further, it is not even *eating* that's the problem, or our enemy. It is our *emotional eating* which is the real problem. We eat for the wrong reasons. The solution? We need to raise consciousness about food, eating, choices, and our default programs. We need to ask, "What am I doing now?"

"Food will never be the most important thing about losing weight. In fact, the reason why you haven't lost weight in the past may be because you've focused too much on it." (Cohen, 1999, p. 131)

Eating intelligence means that we will understand that we will essentially want to follow a balanced, low-fat diet. It's as simple as that. Dr. Edwin Bayrd in *The Thin Game*, said that there are really only four components to any successful program for weight control:

1) Regular exercise
2) Sensible nutrition
3) Behavior modification
4) Diet

In his approach, he argues that the diet that works best is the one that asks the smallest sacrifice for the longest time.

Another critical domain of knowledge for eating intelligence involves nutrition. Fat will make us fat faster. Fat contains more than twice as many calories as carbohydrate or protein. It only makes sense that we should consume less fat. This means avoiding deep fried foods as well as avoiding cooking with oil. It means thinking in terms of fresh vegetables and fruits.

Inasmuch as the human metabolism rate falls one-half of one percent per year after the age of twenty, we must decrease our caloric intake by 5 per cent per decade to maintain a constant weight.

Judy Wardell (1985) in her book *Thin Within: How to Eat and Live like a Thin Person*, provides eight key for weight mastery (pp. 6-8), that she says she discovered when she explored "the magic" of naturally thin persons. She discovered these secrets by asking questions about the eating habits, beliefs, etc. of these people. Then she formulated their "secrets" into the following *Eating Intelligence* keys. While this is not rocket science, it does indicate a basic *intelligence* about the body and how to fuel it with good food.

1) Eat when your body is hungry.
2) Reduce distractions to eat in a calm environment.
3) Sit up when you eat.

4) Eat when you have relaxed your mind and body.
5) Eat and drink things that your body loves.
6) Pay full attention to your food when eating.
7) Eat slowly to savor every bite.
8) Stop eating before you feel full.

When we use guidelines like these for eating, we can play with them by turning them into a checklist and reality check our eating until it becomes a habitual way of relating to food. That's what Wardell did in her book. She took these eight simple statements and put them at the end of each of her 30 chapters as a 30 day check.

Checklist for Evaluating Your Eating Today:
— I ate when my body was hungry
— I ate in a calm environment with reduced distractions
— I ate when I was sitting
— I ate when my body and mind were relaxed
— I ate and drank only the things that my body *loved.*
— I paid attention only to my food while eating.
— I ate slowly, savoring each bite.
— I stopped before my body was full.

The Behavior Modification Frame Game

We can supplement the changes we make regarding *what* we eat with *how* we eat. It's been common knowledge for some time that the following provides us some behavior modifications to our eating habits:

1) Keep a boring refrigerator. Keep a refrigerator that discourages late-night snacking.

2) Only eat in one place. Snacking around the house can be an insidious form of loading up on calories and never noticing.

3) Use a smaller plate.

4) Chew everything carefully. Avoid gulping your food.

5) Plan to fail. You will. Be prepared to take it in stride, and to immediately renew your efforts.

6) Put your fork down between every bite. Take your time. Enjoy the food. Take your time so that your stomach gets a chance to tell your brain when you've had enough.

7) Drink lots of water prior to a meal.

"Keep the Feelings and Lose the Weight" Frame Game

Dr. Daniel Silberberg tells the story of a woman who loved root beer floats in the summer. She had one everyday. Then, when she decided to work on her eating habits and to slim down, she suddnely realized that to lose weight would mean that she would have to stop with the root beer floats. She literally cried when she thought about this.

Why? What did "root beer floats" *mean* to her? She said that they represented to her "summer" itself. "All of the good and wonderful feelings of summer are wrapped up in the very idea and experience of having a root beer float."

When Daniel heard this, he told her that she didn't need to give up the *feelings* of the floats, just the root beer floats.

Consider that. Since *the feelings* occur inside your nervous system as representations, the feelings of the craving for the root beer float won't make you fat. They will only give you a delicious experience. And you can have those feelings without having to act on them. It's not the root beer float itself that creates the feelings or the experience— it's our mind-body system.

You can keep the feelings fully and completely and stay slim and trim and not have to deal with all the calories of the root beer float. Using your power of thought to represent something in all of its sensory sumptuousness gives you the ability to have the experience without the side-effects. The good news is that there are no calories in vivid visualizing.

The Athletic Feeling Eating Game

What if you ate your meals from the perspective of an athlete and while feeling totally athletic? To play this Game, pick a world class athlete that you admire who obviously takes good care of his or her body and *in your mind* step into that person. As you imagine it fully, would that effect what and how you ate? What if you ate from the mind-set of a healthy and wise athlete?

Take time to fully imagine this ... imagine what that would feel like from that frame of reference and the frame of mind that would initiate. As you step into that state of mind, would this be a state of mind that would enrich and alter your relationship to food? Would you like to keep this frame of mind?

Swishing Your Brain to the New Slim You Game

Here's a great Game to play. Next time you question yourself and wonder if you're nothing more than just a fat butt, swish your brain to *the You* for whom becoming and staying fit and slim is "no problem."

1) First, vividly imagine a *You* that's slimmer, fitter, and healthier than you are at this moment. See *the You* as you really want to be: at your ideal weight and taking the actions that make that possible. See the new slim you glowing with health and energy, feeling confident about it, feeling the power of self-control and discipline, etc.

2) Keep editing this picture so that you see *that You* as a three-dimensional life-size image and until it becomes clear and compelling. See the firmness and clarity of your skin, the muscle tone of your body. Keep amplifying it until it becomes so vivid, brilliant that you feel compelled to step into it. You'll know you are doing this right when you begin drooling.

3) Now step into this *Future Slim You* .. From inside, turn and face your future and begin walking inside of this new slim, fit, and healthy body. Experience the feel of lightness, firmness, tightness... walk with the elegance and power of this new body suit.

4) Still within this *New You* for whom losing weight and developing the level of fitness is "no problem," turn around and look back toward the past that has brought you to this place. As you do, notice the steps and stages that brought you here.

5) Now step out of this Future Slim You, and float back into your present day body but only as you bring with you the knowledge of the processes that will lead to this new you ... and letting the feeling of intensely wanting to be there again in that future body pull on you...

Use this *Swish Pattern* to keep cuing your mind-body system about this much more resourceful You who can make it happen. Practice this *Swishing* a couple times a day, until it becomes an internal resource and your mind-body swishes to automatically. (You can discover more about the NLP *Swish Pattern* in various NLP books. See *The Sourcebook of Magic*.)

The Boundaries Frame Game

What boundaries have you set about food?

What boundaries do you need to set about food?

When and where do you say, "This far food, and no further!'"?

The over-loading of food with far too many meanings and values not only leads to *Psycho-Eating,* it also causes us to extend the boundaries of eating so that we over-eat. We then eat for the wrong reasons, in the wrong places, in the wrong ways, using the wrong amounts, etc.

Now we can play a different Frame Game. We can set boundaries for the Eating Game. This enables us to bracket the Game so that it doesn't dominate our every waking minute. In this way, we can protect ourselves against the misuse of food.

When to eat?

Where?

How much?

What and what kind of foods?

In what mood or state?

For what purpose?

Boundaries allow us to know the limits and edges of behaviors:

I know when to eat and when not to eat.

I know what to eat and what not to eat. I have good solid boundaries as well as a warning voice inside that alerts me.

Boundaries also allow us to know when enough is enough. Try on the food as you imagine what it would taste like... and then imagine that an hour goes by, then another. How does the food "taste" during the second hour? The third? How does it make you feel? How energetic or sluggish do you feel?

"Smashing The Wall of Fat" Game

Another Game to play with food comes from Wardell. It involves setting boundaries against fat. To play this Game, begin by imagining your fat as a "Wall of Fat." Imagine it as a wall protecting and insulting you. ... see it, feel it, sense it... As you do, first *thank* that Wall for the job its done for you and all of the positive values it brought you. As that settles, now, what else would you like to say to that Wall of Fat? Have you had enough of it? Are you ready to say *"No!"* to the Wall, to destroy that Wall of fat?

"Extend your hands out in front of you and actually knock it down. Get rid of that wall! Destroy every last bit of it any way you choose... " (p. 169)

Summary

- If you want to play some of the *new Games in town* about eating, *declare* the Games that you're going to play, and begin playing! It's as simple as that. And, as you play and practice at playing, you know that you will eventually become highly skilled at the new Games.

- What new Game would you like to play with food? With eating? Play the *Sensory Delight Game* and learn to really, really enjoy every bit and taste of your food. You'll need less of it if you do.

- As you learn to turn eating and weight management into a Game, it can become a flow experience for you. And when you do that, it makes the whole process here a life-style and fun. It takes the pain and push and difficulty out of it.

Now That You Know—Here's What To Do

- There are a lot of Healthy Games in this chapter that will empower you to become more energized, vigorous, slim, and fit. Which ones will be the easiest for you to establish in your life?

- Use the Frame Game Analysis sheet for establishing a New Game. Copy it and then set up the new Game so that it fits just right for you.

- Ask someone in your life to hold you accountable to making the New Games part of your lifestyle.

Chapter 12

FRAME GAMES
FOR LIVING
WITH ENERGY & VITALITY

- What's your frame-of-reference regarding keeping in good physical shape through exercise?
- What comes to mind when you think about exercising?

He said, "I'd like to have more energy and vitality."

She said, "Really, you really would?"

"Sure."

"Then the first step is to get off your butt!"

"Really? Does it finally come down to that?"

"Yes, it certainly does."

Ah, getting off our butts and exercising. A key ingredient in the Game of becoming Slim and Fit.

Exercising, like eating, plays a central role in our sense of being well, energetic, alive, having vitality, self-confidence, etc. Exercising, like eating, is not just a "physical" thing apart from our frames of mind. Our mind-frames *about* our bodies governs how we feel and act. Since our frames play that much of a role in our everyday experiences, we might as well identify them and transform them so that they serve us well and increase the quality of our lives.

Flushing Out the Old Frames

When you think about *exercising*, what comes to mind? Do you immediately begin thinking about the time, trouble, and effort that the exercise will take? Are those *ideas*, feelings, and experiences your first *reference?* What comes next? Where does your brain then go? Do you entertain any of the following ideas?

Why does exercise have to be so hard?
I'm getting too old for this.
I don't think exercise is really that important.
First things first, I just don't have time for it now.

If these are some of the thoughts that you entertain about exercising, these frames will undoubtedly stop, prevent, and sabotage you from playing any of the empowering Activity Games of this chapter. Frames are *that* crucial. Ultimately, we can only play the Games that we have Frames that support.

Frame Games to Kill the Spirit of Being Active

How well adjusted are you to the undeniable fact that our bodies are made so that they absolutely need movement, activity, and challenge? Do you like that or do you resent it? What frame-of-reference would you have to entertain in your mind, and set in your consciousness, so that you will take better care of your muscles, heart and lungs, posture, etc.? What *Frame Game* do you now play with regard to this?

Ain't it Awful How Out of Shape I'm In?
Wouldn't it be Great to Have a Well-Shaped Body?
Exercise is All a Bunch of B.S.!

"My Healthy; My Life" Game

Without really knowing what I was doing, I happened to set several frames about exercise early in my life that have proven extemely valuable and beneficial. In the book, *Motivation* (1987), I told about finding myself at 207 pounds when I was 25 years old. And at 5' 10", that wasn't good. When I went out for my first "run" (if you could call it that), I planned to run a mile or two around a quarter mile track at a local college. I didn't get 1/3 the way around the first lap without panting and gasping. I had to walk the next three laps to make a mile.

That was it. I thought I was in good shape because I had been lifting weights on a fairly regular basis. But no. I was suddenly shocked into the realization that I had very little cardio-vascular fitness. I had been eating too much, exercising too little, and assuming that skeleton muscle strength was the same as cardio-vascular fitness. I was wrong.

It was that day in 1975 that I made a definitive decision to get back into shape and to maintain it. I pushed hard so that within a six months I was running seven miles daily. Within a year my body weight returned to the 160 to 165 pounds that I have maintained since. For the past twenty-five years I have averaged four or five miles a day and maintained that body weight.

During the past few years as I have conducted intensive trainings, some lasting 7 days, some 20 days. During these trainings I will typically go from 8 in the morning to 10 in the evening presenting and/or working with people. In the past five years, hundreds of people have commented on my unending sense of energy, that my energy level never seems to lag, and that I seem just as fresh and vital on the tenth or fifteen day as on the first day.

"What accounts for your unending energy?"

I know that it depends to a great extent on regular exercise, sensible eating, and the supporting frames of mind that give me a good relationship to eating and exercising.

So, what frames did I set that have given me the ability to sustain a high commitment to exercise for a quarter of a century?

I set a number of them. One of the first that I set was a belief frame about the crucial importance of health and energy. That allowed me to begin playing the *"My Health is Absolutely Vital to Life and to the Quality of my Life"* Game. I believe that. From that frame of mind, I play numerous sub-Games:

> "It's much easier to maintain a healthy lifestyle, than recover it."
> "My health is a sacred trust."
> "Maintaining a healthy body gives me the basis for achieving my goals."

As I set this value frame wherein I began to adopt the view that a healthy body is the foundation for a healthy mind, I increasingly accepted the Greek ideal, "A healthy mind in a healthy body." As I did,

I made that my theme and my motto.

Doing so allowed me to begin playing other Frame Games. For example it allowed me to realize that I could use running, hiking, biking, rollerblading, skiing, walking, etc. as "thinking time" for creative ideas, as "health insurance" (truly insuring my "health"), and as body shaping.

"Exercising is just thinking time" Game.

"Exercising is my real health insurance" Game.

"Exercising is what allows me to shape my body" Game.

"Exercising is de-stressing time" Game.

"Exercising is time to write on the run" Game.

"Exercising gives me the vitality to stay alive" Game.

Later, when I eventually began experiencing the endorphin highs from cardio-vascular exercising, I began playing that Frame Game. This enabled me to begin thinking about exercising as my Game of:

Time to Get High

Time to have Fun.

Time to do something Special and Wonderful.

"Do you always feel like exercising?"

Are you kidding? Of course not.

There are lots of times when I don't feel like it. There's a strange thing about that though. More typical than not, *the very times when* I don't feel like exercising are the very times when I most of all need to exercise. It's also the very times when exercise will do the most for me in the shortest period of time. Of course, when I'm suffering from an injury, a cold, or something, that will not be true. But most of the time, if I can just get my rear-end out the door for a walk or run, I'll be feeling much better within thirty minutes.

So, in the matter of exercise, I have had to learn to develop some good *"Anti-Excuse Frame Games"* so as to not fall victim to excuses. Here the following Frame Games have come into play and served me very well over the years:

"I don't have time to *not* exercise" Game

"The busier I get, the more I need to maintain the fun of exercising" Game.

"I stubbornly refuse to be defeated by a unpleasant mood."

"I can always for a mile walk to see how I feel."

Whenever we attempt to solve a *symptom* like, "not feeling like I want to exercise" or make lots of excuses for the lack of exercising without even considering *the frame* that drives such symptoms, we just waste lots of our time and energy. Our *frames* drive everything. Our frames control our feelings, decisions, perceptions, understandings, choices, habits, and lifestyle.

So without exploring and truly understanding the frames of meaning that govern our exercise behavior, we fail to address the true source of the difficulty we experience. Problems always ultimately go back to our frames.

Yet as we recognize that within and behind every action, habit, emotion, and behavior there's *a governing frame* that directs our consciousness, we then go on a search to find and address that frame of reference. When we do that, then we can locate and use the leverage points in the system to transform the system.

The Proactively Responsible Frame Game

Suppose you decided to play this Game. Suppose you made an empowering decision to make your fitness and health totally your responsibility and that you will choose from this day forward to "insure" your health by exercising regularly. Just suppose that for a moment. What would be the results if you made that decision and began living your life from that frame of reference? What benefits would you accrue to yourself? Would it enhance your life?

Consider the opposite. If you are not an active agent who proactively assumes responsibility for your health, then who is? Who could you delegate that responsibility to—even if you could?

To play this Game, frame some words about assuming complete ownership of your body, of keeping it alive, active, strong, and feasible so that you find this idea exciting and compelling. What do you need to tell yourself that would frame this so that it naturally motivates you? What mind-lines can you invent that would nourish and feed your mind?

"It's the only body I'll get so I'll treat it with honor" Game

If you're not convinced, then do this. Imagine life *without* your health. Imagine it without the physical energy and vitality to take effective action in business, in relationships, in doing the things that are important for you to do. Imagine losing your health to stagnation, weakness, illness, or disease.

If you damage or neglect your health and don't take care of it with proper nutrition, exercise, activity, stretching, strengthening of your skeletal muscles, etc., what will you do for a body? I like this frame: My body is the only one that I'm going to get in this life. Use this frame for appreciating and taking better care of your body. Let it invite you into a new Game with regard to staying active, exercising regularly and sufficiently, and making sure your body gets a good balance between rest and challenge

"Bodies are made for movement and activity" Game
"A Healthy Mind in a Healthy Body" Game

Exercise Intelligence—Aiming to Stay Active

It doesn't take a rocket scientist to realize that our bodies work best when we *do things to stay active*. Our bodies were made for movement and activity. That's what exercise primarily does for us. We exercise to feel alive and vital. The obvious problem that so many of us face today is that we have become far too sedentary. We do not have enough natural activity built into our lifestyle. That's why we have to take charge to intentionally sneak more activity, and more intense activity, into everyday situations. And it's not that difficult. We can take the stairs whenever we have an opportunity. We can park a couple blocks away. We can use our creativity to imagine all kinds of ways of adding more muscular and cardio-vascular activities to our lifestyle.

The more active you are, the more efficient you become in burning fat. *To be slimmer*—we have increase our activity level. This means that we get off our rear-end and walk more, take the stairs whenever we have an opportunity, stand rather than sit, pick things up and carry them, etc.

It's activity, in the form of movement, that changes the body and that sculptures the body. Dieting cannot really do that. In exercising and increasing our activities, we burn fat. We turn up our oxygen consumption, which increases metabolism, and which increases our sense of feeling good. Would you like to sculpture your body? Are you willing to do so using exercise?

Get a brisk half-hour walk everyday if you can do nothing else. Then, whenever you can take a few extra steps, do so. This may involve parking the car further away and walking an extra block, walking to the mailbox, pacing, etc.

"I shall raise my metabolism level" **Frame Game**

Research has also shows that the fit are more efficient at *using* fat whereas the fat are more efficient at *storing* fat. Most of us know that fatness creates a vicious cycle. After all, our body chemistry favors stability. So if we are active and burning lots of calories, our bodies need more and will become more efficient at burning fat. If we're inactive, and dieting, our bodies will shift to storing the fat we have.

By becoming more active, we can actually increase our metabolic rate. After all, as we use our muscles in staying active, the muscles burn fat and this takes oxygen.   With increased activity, our metabolism speeds up. Fat requires oxygen to be metabolized and exercise is what increases the availability of oxygen.

Working out does more than just burn calories, it gives us an "after burn." That is, it boosts our metabolism so that we will be using up more calories for hours *after* we have finished the workout. *Psychology Today* has reported on studies at the University of California that show that the metabolism is still revved up twelve hours after a workout.

Using exercise to raise the body's metabolism may also lower our weight setpoint so that we balance out at a lower weight. To do this, we do *not* need to exercise intensely. That, in fact, may be counter-productive. We mostly just need to stay active and to use our muscles. When muscles are exercised slowly, moderately, they'll invade the fat stores to get moving.

Changing body chemistry takes time. Working out today and looking in the mirror for results tomorrow means you're trying to play this Game *impatiently*. And that will sabotage your best efforts. Exercising intelligence involves thinking long-term, patiently, as you recognize all of the values of exercise:

Exercise is a foundation of youth.

Exercise changes body chemistry, sending nutrients all around the body, supplying it with more energy, infusing it with more oxygen, etc.

Exercise burns fat.

Exercise is a "Fat Burning Pill" (Cohen).

Exercise speeds up metabolism.

Exercise improves health and overall well-being.

Exercise reduces the risk of many health problems (arthritis, back pain, cancer, diabetes, fatty deposits in arteries, heart disease, high blood pressure, osteoporosis, stress and tension, strokes, etc.)

Exercise reduces stress and negative emotions.

Exercises releases endorphins and creates "the endorphin rush."

Exercise improves the tone of your muscles so that they burn fat more efficiently.

Cohen and Verity (1998) write a lot about the nature and value of exercising:

"Fifteen minutes of continuous activity seems to be the time trigger that stimulates production of fat-burning enzymes. The more fat burning enzymes you have, the more fat you can burn." (p. 78)

"Fat people store glucose as fat whereas fit people store it as glycogen which is easier to use. People who are overweight have different fat cells. It's the enzymes in the fat cells that convert food into stored fact. ... By increasing your exercise levels you can actually decrease the level of your fat storing enzymes." (p. 83)

"Comfortable, regular activity is the key. When you diet, you can lose weight, but still have the chemistry of a fat person. When you start including steady, enjoyable activity in your life, your body becomes more adept at burning fat always. Your muscles become more toned so that they develop more of the enzymes that burn fat and the, if you start eating more again that will probably be fine. Your body will actually need it." (p. 111)

To play the *Exercise Daily Game*, make sure that you engage in activities that you enjoy. *Enjoyment* will enable you to make it a regular part of your daily life. *Enjoyment* will make this Game sustainable over the years.

Summary

- As with eating and food, ultimately our attitude and frames about exercise determine how we feel, how we act, how we perceive things, and the quality of life that we experience.
- Do you need to play a new Game with regard to exercise, stretching, lifting, cardio-vascular strength? If so, what new Game would you like to play? What new frames will support that Game?

Now That You Know—Here's What To Do

- What new Exercise Game will you first step up? How important is this for you? Is it important enough to provide the motivation to set up this new Game? If not, how could you increase your motivation? Return to the Intentional Game to get a big enough *Why*.
- Use the Frame Game Analysis format to fully set forth the new Exercise Game that you want to play.

Chapter 13

FRAME GAMES FOR MAINTAINING THE VITALITY OF BEING FIT AND SLIM

Frame Games for Making it Lifestyle

Games in This Chapter
The New Me Swish
No Failure; only Feedback Game
The Patience Game
The Great Long Term Benefits Game

- Would you like to play the Maintenance Game?
- Would you like to make a transformation in your life about eating and exercising, a transformation that you could keep and maintain?
- Would you like to turn your new patterns and Games into your very lifestyle?

If you answered *"Yes!"* to the above questions, then this chapter is for you! Let's talk about how to sustain and make permanent the transformations so that you can keep them for the rest of your life.

"The Me For whom Maintenance is no Problem" Frame Game

We have already played the "Swishing Your Brain" Game. Here we'll do it one more time. Can you now imagine *the you* for whom turning the eating and exercising Frame Games into your lifestyle is no problem? Would you like that? Take a moment and just imagine that.... And as you do, begin to make a clear, vivid imagine of *the kind of person you would have to become* in order to maintain that way of thinking.

If you have any difficulty doing this, think about someone that plays the kind of eating and exercising Games that allows them to persevere and keep at it, year after year, and have a great time in the process. See that person, hear him or her, and when you have a really vividly image it, step inside and feel what it feels like to be that way.

What the mind can *vividly imagine*, the body can begin to actualize. So give your neurology a boost by imagining *the you* for whom playing these Frame Games is a piece of cake.

The "Only Feedback, Never Failure" Frame Game

In every area of life, this Frame Game works wonders. It recognizes our nature as humans in an ever-changing world. After all, as fallible and ever-growing, evolving, and developing persons, it is our nature and destiny to keep learning. By re-classifying the attempts we make that do not reach our goals as great and important feedback, we enter into and begin to play a new Game. No more beating ourselves up, insulting ourselves, degrading ourselves. Now we play it very differently. We look upon everything as a learning experience, and we look upon the so-called "failures" as valuable information. Our next step in play is to simply make a new attempt that utilizes our improved knowledge.

With this in mind, now we can use each eating event as a learning experience. We never "blow" our diet because we're not "dieting" in the first place. We're living a lifestyle of health and vitality. If we eat something that doesn't fit, we notice it and rejoice in discovering how something lured us into the mistake. Using the attempts that do not move us closer toward our goal, or that doesn't quite make it, as an open feedback loop gives us the ability to continually refine our skills. It provides that basis for ongoing development and incremental improvements in the quality of our lives.

Then, using the forgiveness frame, we can simply release all experiences that are past, and move on with life. This is especially true for releasing old emotions, resentments, fears, angers, regrets, etc.

The Patience Game

When we step up to play the Frame Game of *Patience* we adopt a perspective about long term effects. We shift our thinking to consider how we can use incremental steps that keeps moving us closer and closer to our desired outcomes. The American Dietetic Association says that among the keys for lasting weight is to aim to lose one or two pounds per week.

People nursed on impatience typically find that shocking. My friend Nathan is like that. When I first mention that to him, he huffed and puffed and said that it would take him forever to lose his 73 extra pounds.

"Actually, Nathan, I think it will take you 30 to 40 weeks."

"30 to 40 weeks, why that's almost a year!" he said raising his voice and letting his frustration and anger be known.

"Yes," I said, lowering my voice and making it softer. "Just imagine, next year at this time, you'll be at your ideal weight."

"But that's so long..."

"How much did you weigh last year at this time?" I inquired.

"Probably 60 or 65 pounds overweight."

"And the year before that?"

"Probably the same ..."

"So you have been effectively maintaining 65 to 75 pounds overweight for years. So consider the wonder of using the next twelve months to change that forever."

He wasn't convinced. And sure enough, a year later, he was about the same even though he had tried two crash diet approaches. Each time he felt like he was depriving himself and so he bounced back to his previous weight. Each time it felt like such a sacrifice and a lot of hard work.

I'm still recommending that he adopt a more moderate attitude in his dietary change and exercise and to aim to lose one or two pounds a week and to slowly habituate the new lifestyle changes. In that way, it would become *a lifestyle,* and not a "diet" at all. It would become his way of eating and exercising.

This is one of the most difficult challenges for many people (if not most people). In learning to shift from the "Instant Cure" Frame Game that holds out such incredible promises of extraordinary results with little effort, they will have to adopt an entirely different attitude.

To play this Game, we have to shift our outcome frame to aiming for one pound loss per week for a year. That's fifty-two pounds. How much of a difference would that make for you? Find some language to support this: "Easy does it..."

We play this Game because striving to go too fast only sabotages weight loss. It does that, in part, because our bodies have been designed to store fat if they get the impression that there's not enough. It also slows down our normal fat-burning metabolism rate. So shifting to a kinder and gentler approach, one that's governed by patience and long-term thinking, enables us to play a much healthier Game, and one much more likely to succeed year after year.

The Great Benefits Frame Game

Earlier in this work, we began asking the *why* questions. We did that to develop a totally motivating Outcome Frame (and Outcome of Outcome Frame).

> *Why* do you want to lose weight and get to your ideal weight?
> *Why* would that be of value to you?

We need *a big why* for anything that we want to install as an inherent part of the way we think and feel. Do you have a big enough why? Have you fully entered into the *Aim Game?* Since it's important that you do, review, refine and rehearse the benefits you will receive and will continue to receive as you lose weight and feel more energetic.

> "I am strengthening my character by choosing long term benefits."

"Ah, I Understand Eating and Exercising Fitness" Game

How much weight do you lose by merely "intellectualizing" about great concepts and programs? I would not guess that you lose very much. Nor would I suppose it would enable you to eat right or exercise regularly. This does not negate intellectual understandings. Actually, *understanding* does play a key role if we want to play the Game of Maintaining Success.

Truly understanding *how* a process works and why it works, and the mechanisms involved in making it work allows us to *take charge* of the process and to customize it for ourselves so that it fits even better. Here understanding the governing principles for eating and exercising, for energy, weight management, habit creation, etc. allows us to design a program that will fit for us.

Figure 13:1

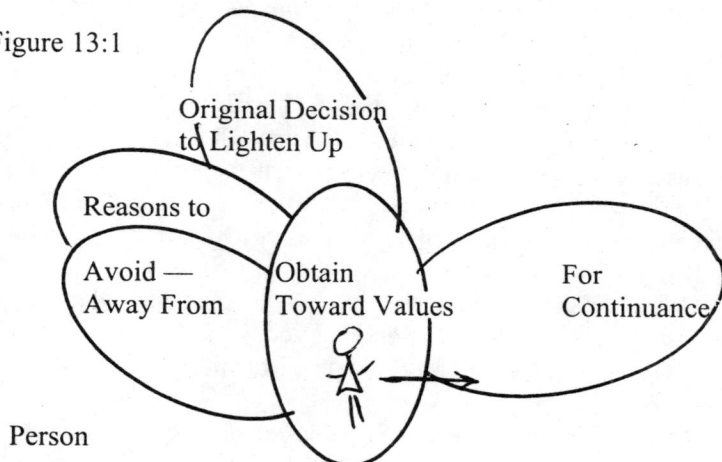

Original Decision to Lighten Up

Reasons to

Avoid — Away From

Obtain Toward Values

For Continuance

Person

Ultimately, the *Slim Game* is played by an appreciation of the fact that we should eat when we truly feel hungry (0-to-5 on the Hunger Scale), we should stop eating when we feel satisfied (5 on the Hunger Scale), and we should notice the energy, vitality, and physical effects from what we have eaten. This *Strategy for Becoming and Maintaining a High Quality Level of Fit Slimness* then allows us to thoroughly enjoy our eating. We concentrate on all of the sensory delights of our food— it's taste, texture, smells, etc. We lose our mind from everything else and just slowly enjoy and savor the food. We separate eating from other activities so that we avoid psycho-eating.

The Right Formula

We need a formula. We need an effective formula. Without the right structure, template, pattern, we will fight against ourselves, the nature of the physics of food and exercise, and frustrate ourselves.

- Has anyone every identified a formula for effective slimming?
- What do we discover when we model people who have successfully lost weight and maintain a healthy lifestyle of eating and exercising?

1) They have developed bi-polar motivations (or mind frames) of a strong aversion and an intensely strong attraction. They play both "I've had enough!" and "Yes! I want that kind of a body and fitness!" Games

They both know what they will no longer tolerate and what they passionately desire. They first got totally fed up with feeling fat and then they became passionate about changing so that they could become fit and lean. For some, their disgust attached such massive pain to being a slob that it powerfully *pushed* them out and away from the old habits. Anthony Robbins writes,

> "The secret of success is learning how to use pain and pleasure instead of pain and pleasure using you. If you do that, you're in control of your life. If you don't, life controls you."

2) *They have developed a strong and committed decision to change.*

However it came about, at some point they made a committed decision that they would look better, become fitter and healthier and change their old habits. They shifted to a new mind frame where they were prepared to do whatever it takes. How about you? Have you entered into that Game, the Game of an empowering decision?

3) *They set a compelling outcome for themselves.*

They shifted their thinking to imagine specifically how they would be when they gained their desired weight and size. They used the principles of *outcome creating* to generate specific, clear, and compelling images that pulled them into their future.

4) *They developed higher levels beliefs which they found most empowering.*

We need empowering beliefs that we deserve to lose weight and look good, that we can achieve that, and that we can anticipate it in our future. What beliefs make you fat or unfit? What would you have to believe in order to become fit and thin? What would you have to believe about food, water, breathing, relaxing, exercising? How strong is your belief?

5) They increased their activity level.
  In this way, their daily activity rate went up, which in turn, enabled them to begin shaping their body in a more desirable way.

6) They learned how to eat only when they were hungry.
  They shifted their mental frame from eating for all of the wrong reasons to eating for all of the right reasons. They gave up the Psycho-Eating Game. They shifted to eating for fuel and energy. Those who have been effective at slimming have learned how to enjoy foods that make them feel good. They have shifted to eating for hunger, and not for anything else. They have learned how to use hunger to trigger eating, and eating only what makes your energy, vitality, and body *feel good.*

7) Many of the effective slimmers made the whole process of becoming fit-and-thin as a "Flow" experience.
  They learned to make it a fun activity in and of itself. This made it something enjoyable and not like work or drudgery at all.

8) They learned how to change their talk.
  They shifted from talking doubt, excuses, etc. to languaging their new thinking fit frame of mind. "I will... I can..." They no longer said, "I'd like to, I hope, I might, I'll try..." They said, "I am totally responsible .." and thereby gave no room for blaming and excusing.

Questions for the "Fit and Thin" Frame Game

Question	*Frame Game*
1) Who do you think is responsible for the changes you want to make?	Responsibility
2) How clear and compelling is the	Vision/ Outcome

vision of where you want to go?	The Aim Game
3) How much do you really want to get there?	Motivation Intentional Game
4) How will it make your life different?	Benefits/ Values
5) How strongly do you believe you can achieve this outcome?	Confidence in Ability
6) How intensely do you believe you deserve this?	Dignity/ Self-Esteem
7) Are you now ready and willing to take action?	Readiness Willingness

Developing a Whole New Focus

Your *frame of mind* determines and governs your focus. The frames in your head set up the Games that you play and what you focus on as you move through life. Throughout this work, I have focused on our *focus* about food and activity. If you have the wrong *frames of mind* about eating and exercising, it will generate the wrong focus— impatiently focusing on the pain of change. Do that and you'll certainly undermine any program.

However, imagine developing an empowering *Aim Frame.* Imagine vividly imagining the slimmer, fitter, healthier You—the You for whom healthy eating and exercising is no problem. When you do that, you shift from the pain focus, the fat focus, the weight focus to the Energy Focus, the Vitality Focus, the Living Life to the Full focus. Doing this also does something else. It takes advantage of the power of the "As if..." frame. We can act as if we have lost the weight and begin to notice the difference in how we eat, why we eat, and our perception of life.

NLP has popularized the saying, "Energy flows where *attention* goes." We have expanded that in Neuro-Semantics in this way:

Energy flows where attention goes as determined by Intention.
In Frame Games, we restate that in terms of Games:
Play flows where the Games goes—as Saith the Frame.

If our focus determines what we will get, then backing up to our higher frames of mind gives us the ability to design engineer the direction and quality of our lives. What *frame of mind* do you most need as you begin to create the body, energy, and vitality that you want?

You now know about the *Games* that you've been playing, and about the *Frame Games* that you can begin to play with eating and exercising. You've been given some conscious understandings as to *why* this works and *how* it works. It's time now to ask one of the most personally crucial questions that we've asked.

What would it take for you to absolutely transform your old eating and exercising habits and install new and empowering habits?

What will it take?

We know that above and beyond everything else, it will take *a change of the way you think*. We know that to become *thin*, and to maintain a healthy life, we have to *think thin*. We have to think in ways that support *thin*, that sets frames so that we can play the Games in life that will result in the payoff of being fit and thin.

The old habits that we will be refusing are loaded with old ways of perceiving things and feeling about things. These create the old programs—the old mind sets, the old mind Games that have created our current habits. These we will have to refuse to tolerate anymore. These we will have to stubbornly reject. As we clear these out, it will provide us new space for installing much better frames of mind—frames of mind that will serve us well and enhance our lives.

So are you ready?

Will you do it?

Summary

- It's not enough to begin to play a new Game, a Game that gives you a fresh new way to think about yourself, your relationship to food, to exercise, etc. In fact, most

- of us have little trouble starting. Staying the course, ah, that's where so many fail.
- That's why we need to learn how to play the Maintenance Game. Then we will keep at it and persist until it becomes our lifestyle.
- Staying the course becomes a piece of cake if we play the Feedback, Patience, Great Benefits, etc. Games.

Now That You Know—Here's What To Do

- Do you have some Maintenance Games established in your life now? What Game do you now play that allows you to persist?
- If not, which Game will you first establish that will give you staying power? Do you have one or more persons set up to hold you accountable for the new Games?

Chapter 14

LINES
FOR CHANGING MINDS

New Frames—New Minds—New Games

When we *feed* our minds *lines*, we nourish ourselves on ideas and understandings that can set frames and initiate Games. Some of these will undermine our success, effectiveness, health, relationships, posture, well-being, etc. When we find *lines*, however, that support the highest levels of our mind, we feed our mind and heart empowering reasons and understandings that positively transform how we think, feel, act, and live. When that happens, *the new Games begin.*

The *lines* that we feed our *minds* empowers or dis-empowers, increases our sense of control over our lives or reduces that sense of control. What *lines* go on in your head? When you eat, over-eat, indulge in things you shouldn't eat, exercise, fail to exercise, etc. what *lines* are coaching you from the sidelines? What lines are hypnotizing you to play life that way?

As you discover and catch the *talk in your head*, you can do something absolutely incredible in terms of human consciousness. You can run a *Quality Control check* on that chatter.

- Does this way of talking to myself, thinking about food or whatever serve me well?
- Does it enhance my life?
- Does it give me more of a sense of control and mastery?

If not, then all you need to do is to begin to feed your mind with some really healthy *lines* that will change your *mind* and enrich your internal mental-emotional world. That's all.

The Meanings of Mind

What is *the changed mind* that will bring about weight loss, weight management, the new habits for eating and exercising in healthy and appropriate ways? It completely alters the current meanings that we give to food and numerous other facets of eating. This will send us to working with and transforming *the meanings* that we have attached to food. Many of these are not even in our conscious awareness. Over the years, various *ideas* have become connected to food (love, satisfaction, reward, connectedness, warmth, etc.) and now these *ideas* operate as our higher frames of mind. That's what "makes" us feel and act as we do—even when our more intelligent mind knows better.

Throughout this book, we have explored how *a frame of mind* works powerfully to establish our way of moving through the world. In the process we presented many powerful procedures for taking total control of our higher levels of mind. And it is in the process of managing the higher levels of our mind that simplifies this entire process and makes it easy.

Conversely, when we do not change things at the highest levels of mind— then changing a primary level habit like eating feels like, and is, hard work.

What makes it hard? How is it hard?

Because we end up fighting ourselves! It feels like a "fight" because it is a fight! One part of us wants something that another part fights. No wonder we experience trying to change habits in that way as hard, unpleasant, and painful.

If *meaning* at the higher levels of mind describes *the leverage point* for change in the human mind-body system, then this highlights the importance of language. Language gives us one of our most important tools for altering meanings and creating new meanings. Traditionally, people have talked about "affirmations" and used them to feed their mind. Yet typically, most don't find that affirmations work very well. Numerous reasons explain that. These mostly have to do with the goal statements *not* being well-formed. For that, they need to be stated in the positive, coded with specific see-hear-feel details, steps, and stages that you can initiate and maintain, and that creates a compelling future and not a false statement about today.

To provide a much more powerful way to use language so that it powerfully affects your mind-body system, your very neurology. So I have devoted this chapter to providing pages of something much more powerful than affirmations, namely, *Mind-Lines*. The powerful new Mind-Lines (as a form of reframing meanings) will give us new way us to frame our minds about food, eating, exercising, discipline, etc. You will then be able to use those lines for changing the fat in your head. (See *Mind-Lines: Lines for Changing Minds,* 2000, 3rd edition.)

Mind-Mastery via Mind-Lines

As you learn how to truly master your mind, and all of the higher levels of mind and to set new frames of mind, you thereby are able to truly master and manage your body and habits. This is essential. To truly become the master of our fate, the captain of our soul—we have to take possession of our mind and use it to guide our life. As you learn to actually possess your own mind, you will find the ability to exercise self-control growing by leaps and bounds. What's the current software in the head for eating, exercising, etc. What kind of new software do we need?

The Motivation to Play

We all know that it takes *motivation* to change anything. It takes a *motive, a reason.* This explains the importance of the *Intentional Stance Game* (the Aim Game) that we focused on in some earlier chapters. As we develop vigorous and robust "reasons," it helps create focus, concentration, and personal power. *Why* do you want to take charge of your eating habits? Your fitness habits? Your health habits? What's driving you?

Motivation involves the feelings and emotions which arise from our reasons that govern *why* we want whatever it is that we want. Where do our reasons emerge from but from our higher frames of mind. The power to get yourself to do what you want to do (what we typically call "discipline") arises when we have developed a new frame of mind about eating, exercising, staying fit, etc. It emerges when we have:

- *An empowering decision* to make a clear-minded choice for being fit and lean,

- *A sense of proactive responsibility* that enables us to assume ownership of our everyday actions,
- *An awareness of current patterns*, and
- *A great and compelling vision* that pulls us into a healthy future

We Reduce the Mental Fat by Refusing Old Games

Most people who struggle with fat and unfitness, with the inability to control their eating and exercising do so because of their *frames*. They have frames of mind that support what they don't want. The fat is first in their heads, then in their bodies. This actually identifies the first thing we have to do. We have to get rid of the fat in our heads. Before we can explore and act on the secrets for becoming and staying vigorously fit and thin, we have to stubbornly refuse the ideas that have supported the misuse and abuse of food and exercise.

"Food as Fuel" Frame Game

- The lure for food is not an irresistible magic spell; it's just food. I don't need to think of it as a magical power, but only as a necessary "fuel" requirement for the body.
- As important as *what* I eat, *how* I eat is equally important. Eating in a relaxed way enables me to enjoy the food fully and treat it for what it is— just food.
- It's not the mounds of food that I eat that give pleasure, but the quality of the food in terms of energy and calories.
- What am I really doing when I go grazing for more food even when I'm not hungry? Oops, there I go grazing again. Baaahhh..
- I eat so that I can move, breathe, talk, and stay alive. It's fuel for life! And that's all it is.

The *"Food is For Hunger"* Frame Game
"It's Just Food" Frame Game

- The pangs of hunger are not my enemy, but signals about my need for food. I'll welcome and celebrate my hunger pangs and distinguish them from pseudo-hunger pangs.

- Feeling hunger doesn't mean I'm going to lose control, it means I'm hungry, that's all.
- A signal, like hunger, is just a signal, and not a command. I can notice, consider, act on it, put it off till later. I have many choices.
- All hunger isn't the same. My so-called hunger at 10 am when I've had a good breakfast, or at 3 pm when I've had a good lunch isn't the same as the hunger after hiking in the wilderness all afternoon.
- Hunger can mean lots of things. And it takes a brain to create meaning, I shall run my own brain to give the sensation of hunger appropriate meanings. I eat for hunger!
- Hunger doesn't mean I'm starving and need to stuff myself, it means that my tank is using up its current fuel load.
- While food has meant a lot of different things to me over the years; from now on I will evaluate it in terms of it's value for energy and vitality, not satisfaction, or pleasure.
- It's not "goodies" it's just food– food for fuel. To romanticize food as goodies is like thinking about gasoline as car "goodies."

The "Psycho-Eating" Frame Game

- I need nourishment and nurturing and these are different processes. Nourishment comes from food, sleep, and exercise; nurturing comes from friends, meaning, significant achievement, and other emotional things.
- What am I eating for? Am I eating for nutrition, energy, and fuel? Or am I contaminating my eating by turning it into therapy— eating for importance, satisfaction, pleasure, comfort, fulfillment, to de-stress, to handle your negative emotions of impatience, boredom, anxiety, anger, etc.? What am I eating for?
- If I am eating for feelings (who eat anxiety, anger, tension, etc.), then I am eating for all of the wrong reasons.
- Food is tasty and good for fuel, but a terrible way to de-stress. I can do better than that; why I could just take a deep breath, hold, and release and repeat for15 minutes.

- Food is tasty and good for fuel, but a terrible way to do therapeutic work on old traumas. I can do better than that; can find a superb therapist and transform my mind and emotions.
- Food is tasty and good for fuel, but a terrible way to resolve compulsions. I can do better than that; I can use thought-stopping techniques.
- I shall learn to distinguish "negative" sensations so that I don't confuse hunger with loneliness, depression, frustration, anger, guilt, shame, fear, etc.
- What kind of an over-eater am I? Am I a depressive eater? Am I an anxiety eater? Or perhaps an angry eater? What about a bored eater? What emotion drives me to abuse food? I wonder what it would be like to be a healthy eater?
- Food is not magical; it's just food and it can't solve my psychological problems.
- What I'm really hungry for is—intimacy, comfort, sex, satisfying work, limits, self-expression, acknowledgment, fitness, to be held, etc.
- I will eat in a non-urgent, non-frantic and non-guilt ridden way.
- As important as *what* I eat, and *how* I eat is *why* I eat. I eat for fuel and nourishment and do so in a way so that I can enjoy all of the tastes, textures, smells, etc. of the food.
- Food may seem like a good friend—always available, soothing, seems innocent, etc., but there are better ways friends than food.
- Using food like a tranquilizer to calm down confuses medicine with nutrition.
- If I find myself eating for non-hunger reasons, I have an excellent opportunity to search for the inner hunger, the hunger of my soul, and deal with that. There's no need to feed my soul with fries and cookies.
- It seems like it's just food, but it's really about food being my best companion. At least that's the way it used to be.

"Aversion to Over-eating" Frame Game
- That's not the smell of something good & delicious; that's the smell of fat— globs of ugly fat waiting to become one with my

thighs.
- More food? Are you kidding? I've already got too much food on my sides and in my fat thighs.
- Excess weight means that people can't see the real person I am. I have felt like a second-class person through the excessive weight, I'm ready to free myself so my authentic self can be seen and appreciated.
- It's not about food, it's about life; it's about not letting life pass me by through lugging around excessive weight, and holding my head in shame, and avoiding mirrors when undressed, it's about taking my life in hand and making life happen in the way that fits my values.
- It may seem unkind for someone to say I'm fat and I need to lose weight, but it's not as unkind as carrying all this blubber around and looking like a fat pig.
- What's really an unwarranted infringement on my basic human rights is ingesting food so that I swell up like a stuffed turkey
- Let's see, perhaps I should eat more of this stuff and become overweight, then I'll be four times more likely to be discriminated against for being fat. Then I'll have something to really feel bad about.
- Eating when I'm not really hungry only trains me to miss the taste of the food.
- Can you tell yourself to do something and obey that command; or have you programmed yourself to rebel in a mindless way?
- If I hide my food and eating habits from anyone, I'm living a life of lies.
- Feeling food frantic at times means that food has me. Welcome to slavery!
- Actually, cramming gallons of food down my throat is an act of violence.

"It's Just a Feeling" Frame Game
- The temptation to eat is just a feeling, not a command. And as a feelings, it will pass.
- A cookie will not control my emotions or send me into a pit of

self-pity, guilt, shame, etc. I refuse to give it that much power over me and my life.

- The trigger that lures me to want more food is just a feeling, and not a command.
- Thinking about all the things I forbid myself to eat only reinforces my thoughts about eating. I shall welcome thoughts about food, about donuts, about banana splits, cookies, etc. and just notice my thoughts and allow them to float on by. I don't have to forbid, I can just notice.
- If I'm ten, twenty or a hundred pounds overweight, any feelings of hunger does *not* mean I'm going to starve. The sense of "starving" are old feelings connected with old programs.
- Emptiness in my life doesn't equate with emptiness of the stomach, and just a feeling.
- Feeling the rumbling of the tummy does not mean that it has to be immediately filled, it's just a feeling.
- It's not about smothering my feelings with food since that doesn't work, it's about learning how to face, express, and/or resolve my feelings.
- If I hold my feelings in and bury them, and then over-eat to tranquilize them, I create two problems: I fail to deal with my emotions as signals and I get fat. Then I have yet another problem to feel bad about, and so another reason to eat.
- Soaring and then plummeting on sugar does not only affect the body, it affects my moods as well. The best way for a smoother mood that's easier to manage, I'll just avoid high sugar foods from the start.
- There's magic in the actual sensations of satisfaction and in sifting through the other sensations that often masquerade for satisfaction.

The "Eating Mindfully" Frame Game
- Conscious of having been unconscious breaks the spell. Spell breakers for Spell binders.
- From what level of mind am I eating? Primary level eating means eating when I feel hungry and need energy to fuel my

metabolism. Eating from a higher level of mind means I'm eating for a psychological reason or pleasure.

- *Where* did I get these ideas and feelings for eating? Although my folks were doing the best they could with what they knew, I don't need to keep acting out that program mindlessly.

- Mindfulness enables me to eat with choice, I will not eat and nibble without awareness.

- Losing and maintaining appropriate weight is a function of my frames of mind, not what I stick in my mouth. What I stick in my mouth reflects my frames of mind. To lose weight effectively involves a new way of thinking about things.

- I shall *set my mind* before *I set any table.* Setting a table without setting your mind about your higher frames of mind about food, eating, exercising, etc. is to come to the table undressed.

- *Food slamming* (cramming food quickly down my throat) does not serve my overall health and fitness.

- While food slamming offers one relationship to food, but not the only, and not the most healthy. I can slow down, smell the vegetables, and eat in a way that nourishes spirit as well as mind.

- Feeding on negative thoughts gives me more than poor digestion, it poisons my mind-body system. I shall observe my mind and quality control the kind of thoughts that I allow about food, myself, exercising.

- It's my ability to change my attitude and to set new frames in my mind that gives me the ability take charge of my mind-body system.

- Fat is as much a state of mind as a state of body. Weight mastery powers come from my ability to run my own brain. I refuse to emotionally abuse myself in a harsh and judgmental way because I haven't yet succeeded.

- While it's fun to be impatient and to demand instant gratification, it doesn't fit for those with higher outcomes that involve a long term goal.

- The more I win the victory of running my own brain and

succeeding in weight mastery, the easier it becomes.

- It's all too easy to eat mindlessly, to consume calories without noticing. Tracking the food that I stuff into my mouth makes me conscious and with consciousness that brings choice.

- If habits sabotage nine-out-of-ten serious dieters so that they go back to their old ways, then I shall make Consciousness my ally until I develop powerful new habits.

- Eat with your mind. Mindless eating adds pounds, plus you miss *the experience*.

The *Aversion of Dire Consequences* Frame Game

- It just looks like a bowl of chips, it's actually another layer of fat on my thighs. As I rethink this choice, is that what I really want?

- It just looks like an ice cream cone, but it's actually a strategy for having a big butt. Is that what I really want to create?

- When I imagine looking back on this moment 5 years from now, how important will this second helping be then?

- When I think about a lifetime of eating fatty foods, is that something I'll be proud of? Would I want that as an epithet? "Here lies The Fatty Foods Eater!"

- Making food this important empowers "food" so that has more and more control of my mind and emotions. Am I really willing to pay that price?

- When you get the end of your life and you look around at all your accomplishments how much will eating that piece of pie mean to you then?

- It's not merely about controlling food and exercising, it's about refusing to aggravate health problems (high blood pressure, heart disease, diabetes, cancer, etc) so I can experience good health.

- Taking the edge off of my edginess by inhaling a dose of sugar may seem to work for the moment, but what price do I pay for it later when I suffer a sugar low?

The Choice Game: "Hey, I have a Choice in This!" Game
"Who's Really in Charge?" Frame Game

- It's not about "can't" lose weight, have you ever seen a fat victim of a concentration camp? Take food away and reduce to starvation diet and everybody loses weight. It's about having the proper motivation and eating and exercising program.

- Calories don't jump off the plate, you have to stick the food in your mouth, which involves arms and hands, not the food's feet and knees.

- What rule forces me to eat *everything* on my plate? I know that's what dad used to say, but did he want me to obey that rule if it made me fat or unfit?

- The smell and taste of food has a seductiveness that shall not be my life arbitrator.

- I stubbornly refuse to think about food that much; it's just not *that* important.

- I am more powerful than the food on the table.

- I am more powerful than the judgments I make.

- I stubbornly refuse to live like a food slave; I'd rather be a master of my fate.

- Choosing to say *"No!"* to dessert isn't being deprived; being bossed around by food is deprivation. I will no longer do subservient bows to every piece of dessert that I smell or see.

- I will not succumb to the demands of a cookie.

- I will not be defeated by my stomach (or habits, advertisement)

- You do have choice about what you put into your mouth, don't you? Or did you abdicate it to a cookie?

- I refuse to continue to be over-looked for promotions because of the weight barrier.

- Just because I have received lots of unhealthy programming about how to think and feel about food, eating, exercising doesn't stop me from canceling out the old programming and installing a new beliefs.

- Just because I inherited the eating and exercising habits which I did from my family doesn't mean I'm without choices about the eating and exercising habits.

- I shall make an empowering decision to create a customized plan for myself to create my new body.
- I will use all my disgusting feelings about letting my body go to make an empowering decision to begin a new pathway.
- It's not about eating, it's about deciding.
- Since a real decision involves taking effective action, the one thing that I will do this day to install my new program for a fit and slim body is...
- Since chucking down large quantities of food in the evenings or over-fills me and prevents clarity of mind and emotion, I refuse to play that Game.
- Since I've made a grand decision to set my goal for a lighter body and a freer mind, I shall look through the lens of that decision before I take any bite.
- Habit has been a formidable obstacle to successful weight loss; choice shall be a formidable weapon in the fight for self-control and dignity.
- Yes, I've been behaviorally conditioned by food, but who is the master— the Pavlovian conditioning I received from mom about food, or my choices?
- The sheer availability of convenience foods, high in calories and low in nutrition value shall not control my eating habits.
- Some foods hum to me, others beckon. But humming and beckon, even whistling, are only sounds. I still have choice.

The Desired Outcome Game
"What I Really Want is..." **Frame Game**
Having a Great Big Exciting and Compelling Vision **Game**
- It's not about being too hard and difficult; everything is easy when you have a captivating vision. Do I have a compelling vision of *"The Slim and Fit Me"* yet?
- One lapse does not defeat a powerful purpose. I will allow a powerful purpose and vision about health and well-being that I really buy into to have the last word. So speak on Vision.
- It's not about finding enough external reasons; you only need a few compelling internal reasons. Depending on things external

to us puts the locus of control *outside* of us, weakens our sense of personal power, competency, and progress.

- Eating and exercising right means that I can and will break through the weight barrier to new levels of freedom.
- As I imagine *"The Slim Me,"* I float into the room, I'm warm and compelling,. I'm soft and sexual. I sparkle as I move.
- It's not about the taste of the food, it's about how attractive I feel in my clothes.
- As much as it's about losing ugly pounds, it's about using my thinner wardrobe that I haven't been able to get into.
- I'd rather feel slim and vigorous with lots of energy rather than stuffed and bloated.
- It's not about losing weight as it is getting off the old roller coaster.
- It's not about eating or not eating, it's about creating a new body and sculpturing new energy that I'll be proud of.
- Yes, I love my hedonism, but even more I love looking slim and attractive.
- Eating is indeed pleasurable, yet even more pleasurable is staying attractive to the opposite sex.
- Curbing my appetite enables me to keep my curves.
- Commitment and perseverance are easy — because I have a big Vision and a Why that's plenty big enough.
- I enjoy the feeling of lightness and reveling in the joy of that feeling.
- The feeling of heaviness drags me down and prevents me from dancing. How can I dance when I'm bloated?
- It's not really food that I want, it's a greater sense of fulfillment in life.
- It's not food that I want; it's something more significant to do.
- It's not food that I want; it's to destress from my feelings of anxiety.
- What's more important than eating is feeling connected to people.
- What's more important than eating is having control of my habits.

- It's not about will power, it's about intention. And it's about intention-of-intention. What My intention? What do I want? Why do I want that? Do I have a *big enough 'why' yet*?
- It's not that my attention gets caught and seduced by something that triggers the 'hungries,' it's that I haven't amp-ed up my *intentions* so that they govern the energy and direction of my attentions.

"What's Really Important" **Frame Game**
- My freedom is much more important than being controlled by food. I stubbornly refuse to give all my power and freedom away to food.
- Comfort is important, but not as important as fitness (health, looking good, being admired for self-control, etc.)
- Wonderful tastes are important, but not as important as seeing my toes.
- What's more important than chowing down? Is that more important thing big enough to empower me with true choice.

The Most Important Thing ... **Frame Game**
- The most important thing in my life isn't what I put in my mouth next, but how I live my life.
- The most important thing in my life isn't eating, but choosing.
- The most important thing in my life isn't eating, but transcending my old habits.
- Food is important but is it important enough to sacrifice my health? Fitness? Thinness?
- Eating is not the problem, *mindless* eating is the problem.

"The Truth About Food" ... *"* **Frame Game**
- It's not about denying myself, it's about experiencing health, fitness, energy, vitality, and self-confidence.
- It's not about another diet, it's about a lifestyle that supports me in being active, taking proactive action, caring about my well-being, and powering up for life.
- It doesn't just happen to others; it can happen to me. I'm not a

mutant of a race of Naturally Fat People. I'm a human being who can learn the Naturally Slim Strategy.

- It's not about *not* thinking about food, it's about developing some other really powerful, inspiring, and motivating internal representations.

- It's not about denial, it's about awareness. It's about truly focusing on what I'm eating and why. Its about focusing on the smell, taste, and feel of the food. It's about noticing fully.

- It's about being nice to myself and to my body. Giving it high octane fuel to run on and foods that make it look and feel good.

- It's not about how fast I can get to my optimal weight, it's about life-long ongoing improvement. I will lose slowly and keep the gains for the rest of my life.

- It's not even about success in losing weight. Refuse to be fooled by success. It's about keeping my weight to its optimal place and about toning my body with exercise so that it will serve me for mental, emotional, and behavioral excellence.

- It's about eating and exercising in a more balanced and natural way. It's about checking out foods to eat in terms of energy, nutrition, balance, and vitality. It's about allowing the taste buds to readjust to healthy foods.

- It's not about what I like or dislike at the moment. I *learn* tastes, I learn my fast food likes and dislikes, and I can unlearn them. It's about the meaning I give to things that ultimately govern my experiences.

- It's not about restriction and denial; it's about giving myself the chance and freedom to use my body in the way it was designed to be used: for movement, flexibility, energy, etc.

- Moderate exercise and eating works to make me slim and fit.

- It's not about food as it is about my *relationship* to food. When Food reigns as a god, it easily becomes a demon. When I treat food as fuel, I take control.

- It's not about discipline and denial, its about identifying the external triggers for eating that seduce me into the Game of "But I Have To Eat That!"

- It's not even about the triggers for food cravings (ice cream, cookies, chips, etc.), it's about *the meaning* I give to those triggers that have created the compulsion. It's about reframing the meaning.

- It's not about denial, it's about developing better choices. It's only a question of using my mind to discover and invent better choices. What one better choice will I invent this week?
- It's not about resisting food or denying myself, it's about breaking an addiction to sugars (to fried foods, to junk food, to X).
- It's not a matter of denial, it's a matter of gaining freedom to play tennis, volleyball, or a morning jog.
- It's not about sacrifice and self-denial, it's about enjoying the pleasures of food as primary pleasures, but not higher level pleasures.
- It's not about deprivation, it's about finding an optimal amount of sugars and fats.
- It's about becoming an explorer of nonfat and low-fat foods, not about denial and sacrifice.
- It's not about self-denial, it's about not joining the rank of the nearly 10,000 Americans who die every week of heart disease, most of which was caused by high-fat, and high-calorie diet.
- It's not about self-denial, it's about putting high-quality fuel in my systems. I wouldn't put sand in my gas tank, so why overload my body with fat and junk food?
- It's not about self-denial, it's really about choosing high quality foods that are low in fat.

The Sensuous Eating Frame Game

- I will enjoy the sensory pleasures of food as I consciously eat and chew every bite in the appreciation of the energy it provides me.
- It's not about how much I eat (quantity), but the quality of what I eat.
- When I chunk it down, it goes right to the hips and other undesirable places. When I slow down, enjoy each and every bit so that it becomes a delicious experience, I gain less and the

eating experience becomes a satisfying experience in and of itself.

- When I rush eating and make it a gobbling, hurry-up event, I miss eating in a quiet and relaxed way that increases the enjoyment.

- I will think about *how* I eat and develop a different frame of mind about *what* I eat.

- I can feel satisfied on less amounts of food as I focus on increasing the quality of *how* of my eating.

- Any fool can eat mounds of food and get little pleasure form it; it takes an intelligent person to eat an appropriate amount and to get lots of satisfaction from it.

- It's not about denying myself the pleasure of food, it's about managing the pleasure of food so that I use the pleasures of food appropriately and not addictively.

- Eating is and shall remain a private joy and dining a delightful ritual; but not at the expense of becoming a fat pig.

- When my attention isn't present in an activity, I miss the experience. Eating without attending misses the actual experience.

- Eating and enjoying the tastes and textures of foods means living and acknowledging in the moment.

- Compulsive eaters just cram food down their throat and miss the moments of satisfaction.

- The sweet or delicious that we experience occurs only in the first two or three bites. After that we really don't "taste" it anymore, and so don't need any more of it.

- Rushing food eliminates the experience of satisfaction. I shall sit and learn to take satisfaction from all of the tastes and smells of the food I eat.

- If I eat and go unconscious; perhaps I should tune into my body and to my food.

- Slowing down the meal gives a chance to enjoy every mouthful and to stop frantic eating.

- Go ahead, spoil a good meal by snacking on some low-calorie foods prior to the feast!

The Feeling Good Game
What Really Feels Good Feelings is... Frame Game

- I used to think that food made me feel good. But what really feels good is Victory, not over-eating.
- Over-eating actually makes me feel stuffed, and that leads to fatigue and tiredness.
- I will go for the best of feelings— feeling fit and trim, brimming over with energy and vitality .
- While food can taste good and give a certain feeling of contentment, taking charge of one's life creates even greater feelings: self-confidence, victory, control, etc.
- The pleasure of the taste of a particular food is good, but not near as pleasurable as the much greater pleasure of being in control, being fit, etc.

The Persistence Frame Game

- Blazing new pattens requires effort and persistence; so what else would I expect?
- I shall be among the successful: I get up when I fall down. It's as simple as that.
- Thinness is just the other side of character. Since character follows perseverance, I will persevere today and choose character.
- I may slip, but I will not quit. The only defeat is giving up, slipping is just part of the Game of getting there.
- It's not a matter of losing weight; anybody can do that. It's a matter of losing fat and maintaining it for a lifetime.

The Intelligent Weight Management Frame Game

- "To lengthen thy life, lessen thy meals." Benjamin Franklin, *Poor Richard's Almanac.*
- When is enough, enough? Do I know? My "Enough" gauge needs to go in for a tune-up.
- Diets do not work; lifestyle works. Forget diets, they will put me on a roller-coaster of losing and gaining. They will confuse my body. I will think "long-term lifestyle."

- I will think "Quality Controlling" my foods for their ability to add to my energy. I will forget foods for meta-pleasures, foods for life satisfaction, foods for any psychological value.

- The design of building a healthy eating map is to improve the quality of your life; not to feel miserable about this.

- I have two royal roads to weight management, I can eat a few less bites and eat more foods that nourish my health; and I can increase my activity level so that I burn more calories.

- I lose control of my weight when I eat too many calories and burn off too few. Healthy weight management involves eating just the right amount of the right foods and living an active lifestyle.

- Eating breakfast eliminates the overwhelming hunger pangs that hit in the afternoon that turns people into ravenous pigs. Trying to *not* eat all day creates a sense of deprivation, and puts me in the throes of a ravenous hunger.

- High calorie, high fat, and high sugar foods do not serve my vitality, health, and fitness.

- I will stop the fat-producing cycle as I shift to more long-term thinking, and commit myself to my own health and fitness.

- I will maintain an eating environment safe for eating and exercising by removing the high fat, high calorie, and high sugar foods. Potato chips and colas will not control my life.

- There's lots of good choices for better eating, low-salt pretzels, fresh fruits, air-popped popcorn, sugar-free cereal, etc.

- I will make my home and kitchen safe for thinness and fitness by removing the high fat and high sugar foods.

- As I devote time and energy into things that increase my pleasure and productivity, I will similarly devote time and energy into increasing my *satisfaction quotient* with eating and exercising.

It's not about—
- It's not about self-control or the lack of it, it's about not having a workable and productive plan.

- I no longer have to accept the idea that I need to starve in order to then have guilt-free eating, that only sets me up for roller-coaster binging and dieting and undermines my health and energy.
- It may seem silly to some, but taking time to plan my new lifestyle plan for eating and exercising empowers me as I create a map for navigating these experiences. Success comes to those who plan, work their plan, keep themselves motivated about the plan.
- The best weight-loss and weight-maintenance guide is my brain.
- I will find foods with lower calories, less fat, less sugar, etc. to increase my ability to better handle food.
- If I don't take control over my hunger, I will end up at its mercy and it's not a nice tyrant! It will drag me to the kitchen and force me to cram things don't my throat that I really don't' want.
- Losing weight and maintaining it might be hard, but it is manageable. Over-indulgence only means I need to learn better management skills.
- Asking someone to hold me accountable for my eating and exercising habits empowers me. It helps me to make healthy decisions and to practice authenticity.
- I've just signed up for active duty in the War of the Waistline, watch out Fat!
- In the War of the Waistline, losers swell up while winners slim down.
- As I clear out the fat in my head, the fat in my body will go as well. Clearly understanding how to eat and exercise reasonably empowers me for long-term, sustainable weight management.
- To over-eat and to under-exercise gives me two critical deficiencies that will undermine my ability to stay fit and trim.
- "There is no known endocrine condition that will give you obesity if you do not overeat." Dr. Gastineau
- Skipping breakfast and denying food all day can activate the "starvation mode" and really mess up my body. Breakfast helps me start the day out right.

- I can keep the hunger monster at bay by simply feeding it small and regular meals.
- It's simply a matter of finding out how much food I need in order to be satisfied and experience high quality nutrients.
- I cook vegetables with imagines, with flair, and with enthusiasm.
- Calories do count, but counting calories is a waste of time.
- I use to belong to the Clean-the-Plate Club; Now I trust my body to know when.
- Sign in Chinese Kitchen: "Eat your Rice, Think of all the children in American eating nothing but junk food."

The "Nice and Easy Does It" Patience Frame Game

- I most effectively lose body fat by increasing our exercise and decreasing calories, aiming at 2 pounds a week over a long period of time. This is the smart way to lose weight and maintain it. It only takes patience.
- I can take baby steps toward establishing a new relationship to food and to increasing my activity level, small steps in the right direction count.
- I will aim to shed pounds permanently by thinking long-term.
- I will make changes so modest that they're virtually unnoticeable. I will sneak a healthy lifestyle into my life.

"Refusal to Excuse Over-Eating!" Frame Game

- "But it's a sin to waste food!" is just an excuse to eat that I no longer buy.
- It's never about genes or being controlled by food triggers, it's about choice. Every time I put food into my mouth I say, "I choose to eat this because... And so that ..."
- It's not about the magical thinking that there's some magical diet, cure, pattern; but about the hard work of thinking about why we eat and developing a better pattern.
- It's not about genetics, it's about a skill Slim is a learnable skill.
- The grip of habit is very nearly as powerful as the vice of heredity.

- Excuses are wonderful things for excusing my over-indulgence. I can blame it on a thyroid condition, glandular problem, hypoglycemia. But in the end, my end is getting bigger.

The *"Enough! No More Excuses!'* Frame Game

- Saying, I "can't" stop myself from my eating pattern!" is just a way of talking. It's an excuse that I will no longer tolerate. It may take concentrated effort and some work, but I can and will break the old unhealthy pattern.
- Making excuses for not exercising, not eating in a healthy and appropriate way is an art. Yet it's a higher and greater art to break through such excuses to live with vitality and energy.
- It's not that I was born fat, *fat* is what we do to ourselves.
- It's not that I've tried everything and will never succeed, it's that I've tried some dumb approaches and have learned lots of things to not repeat.
- Sure, it's genetic! And at the end of the war they found lots of fat people in the Concentration Camps!
- Sure, the calories jump from the food onto your butt! That's why the Germans kept so many of the concentration camp prisoners fat— they let them tour the kitchens.
- Have you noticed that it's always the fat non-exercisers who complain that exercise increase their appetite?

The *"Hell, No!"* Refusal Frame Game

- Saying *'No!'* to foods that don't enhance your life is not big thing, it's actually a little thing, a little word, just a choice that enriches your life.
- Yes, it tastes good for this moment, but how will it taste when you begin to wear it.
- If going off on a negative tangent with cynical and self-deprecating thoughts sabotages my good intentions, then I'll install a Stop 'Sign in my brain and a loud assertive "NO!" to stop that direction.
- I can use my brain to motivate myself to change by becoming crystal clear about the things I will no longer tolerate and those

things that strongly compel me into my future goal.

The Impatient "Fix it Quick!" **Frame Game**

- Quick fix and instant solutions misdirect me from the true art and strategy of weight management and from living a healthy lifestyle.
- Quick fix for instant solutions are more functions of an ego trip than an intelligent way to reorder my relationship to food.
- Impatience will make me fat. The patience of losing one pound a week will make me thin.

The "Learn To Burn" **Frame Game**

- If I want to lose and maintain permanent optimal weight, I have to learn to burn– burn calories by using my fuel for being active.
- Learning to burn can involve very simple little steps, like walking the steps, parking further away, taking walks throughout the day.
- Learning to burn does not mean running marathons, it only means increasing my activity level.
- Learning to burn includes activity learning in the day which then increases metabolism throughout the rest of the day.

Importance

- When I think about losing the excessive weight and maintaining my optimal weight, I begin to feel the sense of pride and self-confidence that gives me.

I'll Get Support and Accountability **Frame Game**

- Since compulsive over-eating runs in families, I will talk out my healthy eating plans with my family and ask for support.
- It's not about self-control, it's about not having the wrong kind too accessible late at night.
- It's not about the lack of self-control over ice-cream, it's about not allowing ice-cream to be available late at night.
- Stuffing one's face late at night undermines good sleeping and

waking up with vitality.

The *Exercise for Fitness* Frame Game

- The active nature of exercise involves me in my own redemption from the "rust" of inactivity.
- Sustained exercise for sustained life-style weight management.
- Exercise is the great tranquilizer. It doesn't stimulate appetite, it normalizes appetite.
- It's not really a surprise that physical fitness is frequently associated with a balanced emotional outlook!
- Why are we not jogging regularly on every city street and country lane when we could achieve for free the weight loss we pay so dearly to achieve by other means? Why does exercise remain the most widely misunderstood and most neglected variable in weight reduction?
- If I want to lose it I have to move it. My body was designed for movement, activity, and exercise, not for chowing down with a bag of chips.
- The easiest way to keep my body in motion is simply to do more of that I am already doing: standing, walking, climbing.
- If fat is stored energy, fuel for activity, then activity enables me to burn that fat. It's not to feel bad about, it's to use.
- When I challenge my physical limits via exercise, I *lose* appetite, eat less, and then lose extra unneeded pounds.
- Exercise of almost any sort is valuable.
- Doing anything is an improvement on doing nothing!
- No activity is so inconsequential that it fails to benefit the body in some way.
- I've decided to exercise the option of exercising as a new option.
- It couldn't be so simple as to increase my level of physical activity while eating in a nutritionally balanced way, could it?
- Exercise is the greatest variable in energy expenditure and therefore in weight loss.
- Exercise is the most efficient method for Girth Control.
- I know lots of people *contemplating* a diet in order to lose

weight, but I haven't seen *contemplation* take a pound off anyone!

The *Behavioral Modification* Frame Game

- The satisfaction that I can derive from food depends *not* on the amount that I eat or my old habits of eating the wrong foods. It depends on my state of mind, upon *where* I eat (the environment that I create or choose) and *how* I eat.
- Eating when I am standing does count! I will sit down to eat and really count it. It creates less deception.
- I will not distract my mind when I am stuffing stuff into my mouth. I will only suffer from Sleight of Food if I do that and that will not leave me sleight of body.
- Keep a boring refrigerator.
- Whenever you say, "I didn't notice that I was eating *that.*" you are confessing that you've been duped by a Sleight of Food Pattern.
- Those who don't control the environmental stimuli that govern eating habits will become victims of that stimuli.

The Truth about Food Game
The *Permission to Be Human in my Eating* Frame Game

- Do I have permission to eat? To enjoy the food you eat? Or do I have to sneak it?
- Food is for tasting, eating, nourishing, for vitality and radiance.
- Hunger is a sign of life and when I lose my appetite for food, my appetite for living follows close behind.
- I will not curse my hunger, but I will celebrate it.
- The choice isn't between thinking I'm flawed and helpless and thinking I'm normal and capable.
- I can trust that I will ... like chocolate, do my best, like to dance, get angry, afraid, impatient, feel overwhelmed, eat, stop eating.
- The courage to love my life is to ask for what I want to keep asking
- I give myself permission to be angry and to express it. The more I express myself in healthy and appropriate ways, the less

I need to express myself by eating.
- I celebrate that I am and always shall be a fallible human being
- When I binge, always binge with consciousness and in the presence of my friends.

HAVE YOU EVER HEARD A LINE THAT CHANGED YOUR MIND?

LINES ARE LIKE THAT. WE CAN ENCODE GREAT IDEAS IN A SINGLE LINE, A LINE THAT GIVES OUR BRAINS CLEAR DIRECTIONS THAT TRANSFORMS OUR THINKING, FEELING, AND BEHAVING.

WHAT LINES WILL YOU USE TO RENEW YOUR MIND AND TRANSFORM YOUR LIFE?

HOW WILL YOU FEED ON THAT LINE UNTIL IT DOES ITS TRANSFORMATION?

WEIGHT & FITNESS MASTERY USING NLP

I trust that you've been impressed by the NLP and Neuro-Semantic approach to taking control of your brain and body. There are many books in NLP on running your own brain. The leaders in the field applying NLP to health, fitness, slimming, etc. that I like are the following, which I highly recommend.

Healthy habits: Total conditioning for a healthy body and mind. By Kathy Corsetty and Judith Pearson,

This is an excellent work that offers lots of specific on becoming much more aware and mindful about what you are eating and how to do a Food Journal to take control. They have many excellent questions for flushing out *why* you eat as you do, the cues and triggers that seduce you into eating when you know better, and lots of shopping and cooking suggestions.

The book is a warm and personal presentation. You will read their own stories about the relationships they have had with food and what they did to gain mastery.

For details on order their book and other facets of their Healthy Habits program, see their web site:

http://www.healthyhabits.com

Slimming with Pete: Taking the weight off body and mind and *Doing it with Pete: The light up slimming fun book* are two books by Pete Cohen and Judith Verity.

In the first book, Pete tells his story as a personal coach and how he got into the *slimming business* and running slimming workshops. That story occurs on the right hand side of every page; on the left hand side, he has summarized principles, sayings, truths, mottos, lists, etc., that summarize the slimming process.

The second book is primarily the training manual for an eight-week program for slimming. Both are easy to read, full of encouraging

information, and ideas for handling difficulties along the way.
  For more information, see the web site:
                 http:\\www.slimming-with-pete.co.uk
  Or the Crown House Publishing. Web site:
                 http:\\anglo-american.co.uk

Think Yourself Slim: A Unique Approach to Weight Loss. By Carol
Harris
          This books presents many facets of the NLP model about
     mental and emotional processing of information, especially the
     perceptual filters that are called Meta-Programs.   Harris
     describes the basic NLP philosophy: "The approach is that your
     experience is largely created by your mind." (xi) "Once you
     know your own patterns of thinking and behaving, you can
     really make progress towards your goals." "Once you get your
     mind working effectively you will be well on the way to
     succeeding." (28)
       As typical of NLP, the book models out why and how people
     become overweight (Ch. 1), the contributing factors, patterns,
     and myths—or as I would say, the Games that Don't Work. Ch
     3 deals with the Meta-Programs of Motivation, Ch. 4 on the
     Aim Game (Making it Real), Putting Plans to Action, and
     Sticking to it.

MORE ON FRAMES
FRAMING, REFRAMING
AND FRAMES OF MIND

If discovering frames (yours and others) fascinates and delights you and if you'd like to continue developing *Frame Game skills*, the following describes some of the literature in NLP and Neuro-Semantics on frames.

Mind-Lines: Lines for Changing Minds (2000 3rd edition)

A book about conversational reframing that presents a model for *the structure of meaning* and how to intentionally shift and change meaning in more than twenty ways. Based originally on the NLP "Sleight of Mouth" patterns, *Mind-Lines* goes much further as it uses the meta-states model for analyzing and playfully transforming meaning.

Adventures in Time (Time-Lining)

A book about the concept of "time" and numerous patterns for thinking about how to code, represent, and play with "time" so that it enhances our lives. Time-lining describes how to engage in empowering time travel and use the time lining patterns of NLP for fun and profit.

Figuring Out People: Design Engineering Using Meta-Programs

A book about the frames of mind that become our perceptual or attentional filters, called Meta-Programs in NLP. This work presents an encyclopedia approach, identifying 51 Meta-Programs as well as describing how to detect and work with them to increase your language elegance.

Meta-States: Mastering the Higher Levels of Your Mind (2000 2nd edition)

A more scholarly approach to the domain of states-about-states and how that each higher states *sets a frame of reference* that then becomes the "attractor," controller, or executive function of mind.

Dragon Slaying: Dragons to Princes (2000 2nd edition)

The first book to popularize the *Meta-States* model. *Dragon Slaying* presents the Meta-States model and applies it to identifying those higher states or frames of mind that create limitations to our resourcefulness.

The Structure of Excellence: Unmasking the Meta-Levels of Submodalities
An advanced book about the NLP "submodality" model and how they actually operate as meta-frames. This reorganization of the NLP model highlights the importance of frames with special chapters on frames for Negation, Backgrounding and Foregrounding, Transforming Beliefs, etc.

The Secrets of Personal Mastery: Advanced Techniques for Accessing Your Higher Levels of Consciousness
A book that popularizes *Meta-States* with a focus on personal empowerment and mastery. Meta-levels and frames are described extensively in this work.

FRAME GAME BOOKS
Games Business Experts Play
What are the Games that we play in business that make for excellence and success?

Games Slim People Play
We all play various Games with food, eating, pigging out, exercise, etc. What are the Games that you play? Who taught you to play such Games? Do they enhance your life, your health, vitality, energy, self-confidence, etc.? Would you like to play some Frame Games that will empower you in these areas?

Games Great Lovers Play
How about the Games you play with loved ones? Do you have the necessary frames installed that allow you to play with others in ways that honor, support, respect, care, and enjoy them?

Persuasion Games
Frameworks for Persuasion— how to use NLP and Neuro-Semantics for more elegance, grace, respect, and power in influencing and persuading people.

Frame Games Workshops have been conducted in New York City, Washington D.C., Tampa, FL., Austin TX., London, etc. See "Training" schedule on the web site for current information —

www.neurosemantics.com

BIBLIOGRAPHY

Arterburn, Stephen; Ehemann, Mark; Lamphear, Vivian. (1994). *Gentle eating: Permanent weight los through gradual life changes.* Nashville, TN: Thomas Nelson Publishers.

Bayrd, Edwin. (1978). *The thin game: Dietary scams and dietary sense.* NY: Newsweek Books.

Cohen, Pete; Verity, Judith. (1998). *Slimming with Pete: Taking the weight off body and mind.* Wales, UK: Crown House Publishing.

Cohen, Pete; Verity, Judith. (1999). *Doing it with Pete: The light up slimming fun book.* Wales, UK: Crown House Publishing.

Corsetty, Kathy; Pearson, Judith E. (2000). *Healthy habits: Total conditioning for a healthy body and mind.* Lincoln, NB: Dageforde Publishing.

Csikszentmihalyi, Mihaly. (1990). *Flow: The psychology of optimal experience.* NY: Harper Perennial.

Csikszentmihalyi, Mihaly. (1997). *Finding flow: The psychology of engagement with everyday life.* NY: HarperCollins, Basic Books.

Hall, L. Michael (1995/2000). *Meta-States: Managing the higher levels of your mind.* Grand Jct. CO: N.S. Publications

Hall. L. Michael. (1996/2000). *Dragon slaying: From dragons to princes.* Grand Jct. CO: N.S. Publications

Hall, L. Michael; Bodenhamer, Bob. (1997/2000). *Mind-Lines: Lines for changing minds.* Grand Jct. CO: N.S. Publications

Hall, L. Michael; Bodenhamer, Bob. (1997). *Figuring out people: Design engineering using meta-programs.* Wales, UK: Crown House Publications.

Hall, L. Michael (2000). *The Secrets of personal mastery: Advanced techniques for accessing the higher levels of consciousness.* Wales: UK: Crown House Publications.

Hall, L. Michael. (2000). *Frame games: Persuasion Elegance— Winning at the games of life.* Grand Jct. CO: N.S. Publications.

Harris, Carol. (1999). *Think yourself slim: A unique approach to weight loss.* Shaftesbury, Dorset: UK: Element Books Limited.

Laverty, Frank T. (1977). *The O.K. way to slim: Weight control through transactional analysis.* NY: Grove Press. Inc.

Polivy, Janet; Herman, C. Peter. (1983) *Breaking the diet habit: The natural weight alternative.* NY: Basic Books, Inc., Publishers.

Roth, Geneen. (1984) *Breaking free from compulsive eating.* NY: Penguin Books, a Signet book.

Solomon, Neil. (1971). *The truth about weight control: How to lose excess ponds permanently.* NY: Dell Publishing Co. Dr. Neil was the researcher who first named and described the "yo-yo" effect of dieters.

Wardell, Judy. (1985). *Thin within: How to eat and live like a thin person.* NY: Harmony Books.

THE AUTHOR

L. Michael Hall, Ph.D.
P.O. Box 8
Clifton, Colorado, 81520 USA
(970) 523-7877
Michael@neurosemantics.com
www.runyourownbrain.com

Dr. L. Michael Hall earned his doctorate in Cognitive-Behavioral Psychology with a special emphasis in psycho-linguistics. He has long been interested in the structure of "mind" and developing practical models and tools for providing more freedom, mastery, and power in taking charge of our own minds. His dissertation dealt with the *languaging* of four psychotherapies (NLP, RET, Reality Therapy, Logotherapy) using the formulations of General Semantics.

After many years as a psychotherapist in private practice, Dr. Hall began running trainings in assertiveness, negotiations, conflict management, anger control, and then NLP. After studying with Richard Bandler in the late 1980s, he began modeling and developed *the Meta-States Model* (1994) while modeling *resilience*.

As a prolific writer, Michael has written over 30 books including *The Spirit of NLP, Becoming a more Ferocious Presenter, Dragon Slaying, Meta-States, Mind-Lines, Figuring Out People, The Structure of Excellence, Frame Games,* etc.

Today as a psychologist and entrepreneur, Dr. Hall lives in the Colorado Rocky Mountains where he writes, travels internationally on behalf of the *The International Society of Neuro-Semantics* and continues to create new models.

Books:

Meta-States: Managing the higher states of your mind (2000)

Dragon Slaying: Dragons to Princes (2000, 2nd edition)

The Spirit of NLP: The Process, Meaning & Criteria for Mastering NLP (1996)

Languaging: The Linguistics of Psychotherapy (1996)

Patterns For "Renewing the Mind" (w. Dr. Bodenhamer) (1997)

Time-Lining: Advance Time-Line Processes (w. Dr. Bodenhamer) (1997)

NLP: Going Meta—Advanced Modeling Using Meta-Levels (2001)

Figuring Out People: Design Engineering With Meta-Programs (w. Dr. Bodenhamer) (1997)

A Sourcebook of Magic (formerly, How to Do What When (w. B. Belnap) (1999)

Mind Lines: Lines For Changing Minds (w. Dr. Bodenhamer) (1997, 2002).

Communicational Magic for the 21st. Century (2001).

Meta-States Magic: formerly the MS *Journal* (97, 98, 99)

The Structure of Excellence: Unmasking the Meta-Levels of Submodalities (Hall and Bodenhamer, 1999)

Instant Relaxation (1999, Lederer & Hall)

The User's Manual of the Brain (1999, w. Bodenhamer)

Secrets of Personal Mastery (2000)

Frame Games: Persuasion Elegance (2000)

The Structure of Personality: Modeling "Personality" Using NLP and Neuro-Semantics. (Hall, Bodenhamer, Bolstad, and Harmblett, 2001)

Games Slim and Fit People Play (2001)

Games Business Experts Play (2002)

The Matrix Model (2002).

User's Manual of the Brain, Volume II (2003 Hall & Bodehanmer) The Master Practitioner Course.

MovieMind (2003).

TRAININGS

NLP TRAININGS
Meta-NLP Practitioner:
An intensive 7-day training in the Essential NLP Skills. This training introduces NLP as a model for discovering the structure of human functioning with a focus on *how to run your own brain* and to manage your own states. Learn the basic rapport-building, listening, and influence skills of NLP, as well as how to access and manage states through anchoring, reframing, and using dozens of NLP patterns. Discover how to use language both for precision and hypnotic influence. Required reading, *User's Manual for the Brain* and *The Sourcebook of Magic.*

Meta-Masters NLP Practitioner:
An intensive 13-Day Training in mastering all three of the meta-domains of NLP: Language (Meta-Model), Perception (Meta-Programs) and States and Levels (Meta-States). This training focuses on the pathway to mastery and how to develop the very spirit of NLP—curiosity, accelerated learning, flexibility, confidence, passion, playfulness, etc.

Basic Meta-State Trainings
Accessing Personal Genius (The 3 day Basic).
Introduction to Meta-States as an advanced NLP model (3 days). This training introduces and teaches the *Meta-States Model* and is ideal for NLP Practitioners. It presupposes knowledge of the NLP Model and builds the training around accessing the kinds of states that will access and support "personal genius."

Basic Meta-States in two other Simplified forms:
1) Secrets of Personal Mastery: Awakening Your Inner Executive.
This training presents the power of Meta-States *without* directly teaching the model as such. The focus instead shifts to *Personal Mastery* and the *Executive Powers* of the participants. Formatted so that it can take the form of 1, 2 or 3 days, this training presents a simpler form of Meta-States, especially good for those without NLP background or those who are more focused on Meta-States Applications than the model.

2) Frame Games: Persuasion Elegance.
The first truly *User Friendly* version of Meta-States. Frame Games provides practice and use of Meta-States in terms of frame detecting, setting, and changing. As a model of frames, Frame Games focuses

on the power of persuasion via frames and so presents how to influence or persuade yourself and others using the Levels of Thought or Mind that lies at the heart of Meta-States. Designed as a 3 day program, the first two days presents the model of Frame Games and lots of exercises. Day three is for becoming a true Frame Game Master and working with frames conversationally and covertly.

Meta-States Gateway Trainings

1) Wealth Building Excellence (Meta-Wealth).

The focus of this training is on learning how to think like a millionaire, to develop the mind and meta-mind of someone who is structured and programmed to create wealth economically, personally, mentally, emotionally, relationally, etc. As a Meta-States Application Training, Wealth Building Excellence began as a modeling project and seeks to facilitate the replication of that excellence in participants.

2) Selling and Persuasion Excellence (Meta-Selling).

Another Meta-States Application Training, modeled after experts in the fields of selling and persuasion and designed to replicate in participants. An excellent follow-up training to Wealth Building since most people who build wealth have to sell their ideas and dreams to others. This trainings goes way beyond mere Persuasion Engineering as it uses the Strategic Selling model of Heiman also known as Relational Selling, Facilitation Selling, etc.

3) Mind-Lines: Lines for Changing Minds.

Based upon the book by Drs. Hall and Bodenhamer (1997), now in its third edition, Mind-Line Training is a training about Conversational Reframing and Persuasion. The Mind-Lines model began as a rigorous update of the old NLP "Sleight of Mouth" Patterns and has grown to become the persuasion language of the Meta-State moves. This advanced training is highly and mainly a linguistic model, excellent as a follow-up training for Wealth Building and Selling Excellence. Generally a two day format, although sometimes 3 and 4 days.

4) Accelerated Learning Using NLP & Meta-States (Meta-Learning).

A Meta-State Application training based upon the NLP model for "running your own brain" and the Neuro-Semantic (Meta-States) model of managing your higher executive states of consciousness. Modeled after leading experts in the fields of education, cognitive psychologies, this training provides extensive insight into the Learning States and how to access your personal learning genius. It provides specific strategies for various learning tasks as well as processes for research and writing.

5) Defusing Hotheads.

A Meta-States and NLP Application training for handling hot, stressed-out, and irrational people in Fight/Flight states. Designed to "talk someone down from a hot angry state," this training provides training in state management, first for the skilled negotiator or manager, and then for eliciting another into a more resourceful state. Based upon the book by Dr. Hall, *Defusing Strategies (1987),* this training has been presented to managers and supervisors for greater skill in conflict management, and to police departments for coping with domestic violence.

6) Instant Relaxation.

A practical NLP and Meta-States Application Training designed to facilitate the advanced ability to quickly "fly into a calm." Based in part upon the book by Lederer and Hall (Instant Relaxation, 1999), this training does not teach NLP or Meta-States, but coaches the relaxation skills for greater "presence of mind," control over mind and neurology, and empowerment in handling stressful situations. An excellent training in conjunction with Defusing Hotheads.

7) Games for Mastering Fear.

To play the Game of Fear, a person has to run his or her brain in a certain way using special frames. The same is true for mastering fear—the power of transformation lies in knowing how to identify the right frames and set them at the higher levels of our mind. This training uses the very best of NLP and Neuro-Semantic patterns to provide true mastery over any kind of fear that might sabotage or limit living up to our Visions and Values. Based upon the book by this title by Hall and Bodenhamer.

8) Games For Mastering Stuttering (Blocking).

There's a structure to the meta-state experience called "stuttering." It is blocking our non-fluency and layering it with a painful kind of self-consciousness. There's also a structure to mastering that experience and moving toward a less semantically over-loading. This training is based on NLP and Neuro-Semantic patterns and structured according to the 7 Mind Matrix model.

9) Games Business Experts Play.

Succeeding in business necessitates developing a certain expertise and business wisdom about oneself, others, skills, markets, finances, managing, etc. Those who do it best, the experts, have a strategy and a certain set of frames of mind that allow them to play those Games. Based upon the book by this title, this training invites you to set the kind of frames of mind and meaning that will bring out your business expertise.

10) Games Slim and Fit People Play.

How do they do it? How do some people relate to eating and exercising in such a way that it is "no problem" to them? What are the frames and games that slim and fit people play so that food does *not* dominate their lives and so that they have plenty of energy and vitality? That's the focus of this training, based on the book by the same title. The training offers specific guidance about how to stop psycho-eating and to develop a much better relationship to both food and movement.

Advanced Neuro-Semantic Trainings

Advanced Modeling Using Meta-Levels.

Advanced use of Meta-States by focusing on the domain of modeling excellence. This training typically occurs as the last 4 days of the 7 day Meta-States Certification. Based upon the modeling experiences of Dr. Hall and his book, *NLP: Going Meta— Advanced Modeling Using Meta-Levels,* this training looks at the formatting and structuring of the meta-levels in Resilience, Un-Insultability, and Seeing Opportunities. The training touches on modeling of Wealth Building, Fitness, Women in Leadership, Persuasion, etc.

Advanced Flexibility Training.

An advanced Neuro-Semantics training that explores the riches and treasures in Alfred Korzybski's work, *Science and Sanity.* Originally presented in London (1998, 1999) as "The Merging of the Models: NLP and General Semantics," this training now focuses almost exclusively on *developing Advanced Flexibility* using tools, patterns, and models in General Semantics. Recommended for the advanced student of NLP and Meta-States.

Neuro-Semantics and NLP Trainers Training.

An advanced training for those who have been certified in Meta-States and Neuro-Semantics (the seven day program). This application training focuses the power and magic of Meta-States on the training experience itself—both public and individual training. It focuses first on the trainer, to access one's own Top Training States and then on how to meta-state or set the frames when working with others in coaching or facilitating greater resourcefulness.

Neuro-Semantics Coaching Certification Training.

An advanced 7 day Training for those with Meta-NLP training and preferably *Personal Genius.* Based on the 7 Matrices Model that arose from *Frame Games* which arose from *Meta-States,* this model ties all of the patterns in NLP and Neuro-Semantics together into a package that allows a person to coach and/or do therapy with these patterns.